The Fountain

Also by Don Cupitt and available from SCM Press

The Fountain

A Secular Theology

Don Cupitt

scm press

© Don Cupitt 2010

Published in 2010 by SCM Press
Editorial office
13–17 Long Lane,
London EC1A 9PN, UK

SCM Press is an imprint of Hymns Ancient and Modern Ltd
(a registered charity)
13A Hellesdon Park Road
Norwich NR6 5DR, UK

www.scm-canterburypress.co.uk

British Library Cataloguing in Publication data

A catalogue record for this book is available
from the British Library

978-0-334-04395-9

Typeset by the *Church Times*

Printed and bound by CPI Antony Rowe, Chippenham, Wiltshire

Contents

To the Members of Sea of Faith
with my gratitude

Introduction

The subtitle of this book is a deliberate tease, for it is certainly not a theology in the traditional sense. In recent years I have, among other things, been attempting to create a new kind of secular and non-metaphysical religious thought. The aim here is to show how great swathes of our experience can be brought together and unified under a single powerful reconciling symbol in a way that can help us greatly by consoling us, by helping us to make overall sense of life, and by showing us how we would do best to live. The central unifying symbol in this present account is the Fountain, but a number of others would also do the trick. They include the Sun, the Fire and Life. Some may wish to argue for the symbol 'God', but for our present purpose the Fountain is very cool and clear.

The main reason for this is that modern scientific theory and modern communications technology have combined to create in all of us an acute awareness of our own, and of everything else's, rushing transience. Everything – the cosmos, communications, life in general, and the self in particular – pours out and passes away. It is not surprising that so many people (especially men) are acutely aware of death; and that so many others (especially women) put a great deal of effort into combating the passage of time.

In such a culture, acutely aware of time, death, and metaphysical lack, what form might religion take? In this book I suggest that there cannot be One True Religion in quite the old way, but we may be able to unify our experience and find religious happiness in the midst of pure rushing transience by contemplating the old religious symbol of the Fountain. Whether in a city square or in a garden, the Fountain is a focal symbol, sited at a point where many ways meet. As an object, it is all foaming transience; but it is surprisingly calming and peaceful to contemplate. It is living water, a symbol of life's ceaseless self-renewal. It is associated with healing and repose. Although it is only a symbol, and there is nothing metaphysical about it, perhaps it may be able to do for us some of the things that God used to do?

Some knowledgeable Roman Catholic theologians may recognize in this the heresy that they call 'dogmatic symbolism', an extremist and impermissible version of the well-established principle that all theological statements are symbolic (or 'analogical'). Maybe: but please give me a hearing first. If my account makes sense, it could have very wide application. And at least it will have shown us what religion can still be nowadays, and how a fully self-aware and critical religion might work.

In the account I give, you will notice that at least some elements of the traditional Christian scheme of thought do remain. The most obvious one is the attempt to combine a general account of the human situation (cosmology/the doctrine of Creation) with a general account of how we human beings should learn to live (ethics/the doctrine of reconciliation or redemption), the two being held together by a single unifying symbol, the Fountain.

In the text that follows you will, however, find that I am wary of using the words God or Jesus. In fact, I am now very doubtful about both. In the case of God, there is the very strong association between the basically masculine, transcendent, legislating God of our 'Abrahamic' group of religions and the historic subjection of women: the transcendent lawgiver God *rules* over Nature and over the human soul, in a way that makes it seem only natural that man should correspondingly rule over woman (she being closer to Nature) and that man should also have the right to lay down the law about what she may and may not do. But today it seems clear that, for reasons Darwinian, environmental and feminist, we need a purely immanent religious vision that can reconcile us to our own complete immersion in time and contingency, and to our own mortality. The Fountain does very well for that purpose, because of the way it combines rushing contingency with life's consoling perpetual self-renewal, while also avoiding any excessive masculinism and transcendence.

As for Jesus, my first problem is that I find it hard now to call myself a Christian, because the word Christian presupposes acceptance of the title 'Christ', or Messiah, which in its turn presupposes a complex supernatural theology of history that nobody should believe in nowadays. I do not care for messianism of any kind. As a result, I'm in an awkward position. I very greatly admire Jesus, but for his sake I must not give him any special supernatural status. Like the Buddha, he was an ordinary man who just happened to be an intensely committed and gifted ethical thinker and teacher. Each of them found and taught a very important and attractive way of life and path to happiness. But Buddhists like Nagarjuna have recognized that in theory there may well have been other unknown Buddhas who have made the same discovery quite independently; and similarly there may well be other human beings who have made an independent discovery of Jesus's ethical Way. So my updated version of Christianity, while it does mention Jesus and has learnt a great deal from him, cannot make him structurally essential to its whole scheme of thought. As John Stuart Mill once sensibly put it, where Jesus was right and we can see that he was right, we can simply thank him and move on. We don't need to keep him as an *authority*; indeed, his own doctrine forbids us to treat him as an authority. As he says, you are not a fully moral person until your living has become completely wholehearted, autonomous and spontaneously generous. You must reject any and every kind of ethics of law, because no *external* constraint upon your behaviour can ever make you a truly moral being. You must live from and by your own heart, and you must go beyond ordinary 'justice'.

For this reason, I admire Zarathustra's saying 'Don't follow me: follow yourself!' I admire the Buddhist saying: 'If you meet the Buddha on the road, kill him!' And I admire the saying of Jesus; 'What goes into you can't defile you: what comes out of you can.' Out of the remote past, we hear a voice commending the sort of frank, direct and warm love of life and of the fellow human being that might nowadays be described as 'emotional intelligence'.

A further difficulty about the name of Jesus is this: all our ancient faiths are infected by the old belief in verbal magic. 'Ours is the One True Faith because we address the right God by the right name, using sacred passwords and powerful spells given exclusively to us by him.' Most radical theologies in the West since Hegel have recognized the need to give up *supernatural beliefs*, but I guess that nobody – other than, perhaps, Hegel himself – has sufficiently recognized the need to give up *the claim to possess the exclusive franchise*: 'You worship God in your way, and I worship him in his.' But I *do* give up that claim, which is why this is only *a* secular theology. It's all true, because it makes no non-rational claims and it does successfully meet what is today our most urgent religious need; but it is *not* the One True Faith. The very notion of a single form of words that gets It All absolutely right is wrong, deeply wrong. Sadly, therefore, I have had to give up the name of Jesus, because it has for so long been claimed that he is the only Way to God and that the Church is entirely justified in setting up roadblocks where it takes fees, as we travel along the Way.

Some of my most recent books (*The Old Creed and the New*, 2006; *Impossible Loves*, 2007; *Above Us Only Sky*, 2008; *The Meaning of the West*, 2008; *Jesus and Philosophy*, 2009; *Theology's Strange Return*, 2010; and *A New Great Story*, 2010) have been casting about, looking for the best way to frame a final brief statement. Here it is then – though no doubt I shall soon start to feel very dissatisfied with it. My chief problem during this past 40-odd years of very intensive thinking and writing has been that we humans now seem to be permanently stuck with a restlessly dissatisfied critical mentality that can never be content with anything for long.

I have been experimenting furiously, looking for a new religious outlook in an age in which it is perhaps no longer possible for any of us ever to find a permanent spiritual home.

And so, farewell ... for now, at least. Thanks to the members of Sea of Faith, and to Linda Allen.

D. C.

Cambridge, 2010

1

The Religious Question

Suppose that we were to feel the need to make an entirely new beginning. We would have to set aside all our received religious traditions and ideas, and begin instead with a universal and purely rational account of the world and the human condition. We aim to be as strict, as up-to-date and illusion-free, as well-informed and as clear-eyed as it is possible to be. Then we ask: Is it possible to join up all the various strands in this account by bringing them under a great unifying symbol that will both make us happy just to be parts of all this, and *also* will show us how we should live?

Yes, I answer. In modern thought, especially since the 1960s, people's outlook has become almost completely non-metaphysical. Our life does not rest upon or within any fixed framework, whether of metaphysical principles or eternal values. There is only 'all this' – and all this is just an ambivalent stream of appearances, continually pouring out and passing away. Everything is on show, and there is *only* the passing show. Everything is contingent, everything is temporal, everything is interconnected, everything is 'relative', everything is mediated to us by, and remains suspended within, the endless shifting movement of our language, and everything is transient. We humans are simply part of the general flux of all things, ourselves continually pouring out into expression and passing away; but our speciality is that our creative outpouring feeling, as it mingles with everything, continually strives to *interpret* the world by reading it, turning it into language and evaluating it. Around ourselves we generate a value-rich communal human life-world, the house of meaning that we live in, but it is never quite as stable as we might wish, because we are continually debating it, revaluing it, and renegotiating it as we go along. In my own jargon I call our life thus viewed 'the fray', and insist that most of us love it – and quite reasonably so, there being nothing else. For us, *our* world *has* to be *the* world – for which the slogan is: 'All this is all there is'.

The world in which we human beings live today is thus a post-metaphysical world in which there is no eternal, enduring and objective Being, no objective and unchanging Truth, and no objective and finally authoritative standard of Value. Everything is permanently in flux, pouring out and passing away – and yet also *on the table*, being negotiated. Everything is always on the move, loved by some and contested by others.

How has all this happened? Until after the European Enlightenment and the French Revolution, most of us (at least in Christendom, Jewry and Islam) thought in terms of a metaphysics of substance. We tended to think of everything first and foremost as a noun, and only secondly started to think of it as doing a bit of verbing. Our assumption, derived ultimately from Greek (and perhaps before that, from Bronze-Age) thought, was that reality is an ordered array of real things, things that are relatively independent, with stable and unchanging natures. Both in the case of being and in the case of truth, we tended to equate objectivity with independent reality and with timelessness. Real being was unchanging, and the idea of time only came in when one was forced to consider something as getting mixed up with other things, and so becoming liable to corruption. Meanwhile, time was on the back burner, in obscurity. If we wanted to think about temporality, we took up something we pictured as ready-made, and mentally dropped it into flowing time just as one drops a stone into a river. Its being in time was just a contingent extra fact about a thing. Especially in the case of human beings, our life in time was like a short period of service overseas. I was my simple and immortal rational soul. Then for a lifetime I was united with a body that was subject to time and – 'therefore' – to corruption. Then it was time for me to be demobbed, and I came back home to eternity with much relief. I was back with God and the angels,

2

in the blessed state of timelessness and eternal life. *Sōma sēma*, the body is a tomb, they said: bodily life here below is a state of 'temporary temporality', a state of alienation and institutional entombment, such as I knew when I was a numbered man, a young National Service officer serving his term overseas from 1955 to 1957. Have you noticed in *modern* English that the word 'time' is used to mean 'a stretch', a term of imprisonment? That is how the old metaphysics of substance led us to think of time. It gave us the idea of life after death as a consolation and a release; but this life? – this life was a *drag*, a burden. One would be glad to be freed from it.

When did everything change? Nothing is certain in the history of ideas, but roughly speaking it was during the eighteenth century that the great discovery of time took place. People gradually began to think that Moderns like Sir Isaac Newton had surpassed the achievements of the Ancients, and therefore that human beings generally might be capable of superseding their own past. The ideas of a universe in ceaseless motion, of historical change, of historical period, and of an evolving 'climate of opinion' or 'spirit of the age' soon followed. More and more, we begin to think of ourselves as being embedded not in eternity but in our own historical period. Looking back, I recognize that the 1950s Cupitt was still orthodox, eternity-oriented and unreconstructed. In world-view he was even a Neo-Thomist, and quite different from the questioning Sixties Cupitt, who was learning fast from Kant and Hume, Mansel and Kierkegaard. And so on, until by the mid-Nineties I was coming into my own final outlook and trying to draw all the threads together. I was beginning to understand that although my own ideas seem final to me, in the sense that this is as far as I am ever going to be able to take them, they will *not* seem final to other people. Not even the statement that 'Nothing is final' is final. If anyone ever does look at what I have done, they will in appropriating it all take it up into a different totality, and perhaps develop it in a new direction of which I can have no prevision. Philosophy, too, is only an ever-changing process, endless talk. I cannot hope to do more than make a small contribution to the ongoing conversation.

So I come to understand that I *am* my own transience, I *am* my own living of my own life, I am just this historically embedded process and not any kind of substance. I am a chain of events and exchanges. I am not an immortal soul, I am a human life towards the end of its eighth decade. I am a verb, not a noun, and I am nearly over. Soon, the play will end – for me, at least. At this stage of the game, talk of there being any 'more' for me is absurd. I'd better start counting my blessings and living in and for the Now, because my future prospects are negligible. Looking around me, I observe that nearly all of my contemporaries have similarly given up any thoughts of 'life after death', because they too know that the very idea is now absurd. Everything is transient, including me, and you, and including even the doctrine stated in this sentence. (Compare the Buddhist doctrine of 'the emptiness of Emptiness'.) Nothing can be pinned down firmly or permanently any more, because there is no firm substance or Ground out there to pin it to.

By such considerations as these, modern philosophy has come to a fresh appreciation of the radical temporality of all being. All beings are 'in be-ing', parts of the flux. Outsidelessly, everything is passing, including us and anything we can hope to produce. Our continuing desire to find something Absolute to cling to is now not our salvation, but our problem. We need to be cured of it.

Thus the prime religious question today is about how we can find 'religious meaning', or 'eternal life', in a world in which everything – all being, truth and value – is secondary, language-mediated, contingent and utterly transient. In traditional discussions of the subject it was said that there are three main kinds of evil, namely Sin, Pain, and Death: that is, Moral Evil, Physical Evil, and Metaphysical Evil, or Finitude.[1] Of these three,

---

1 See G. W. Leibniz, *Theodicée*, 1710; and John Hick, *Evil and the God of Love*, London: Macmillan and New York: Harper and Row, 1966.

it was Sin, or moral evil, that seemed most important to people who lived in a religion-based culture. Then, in the more science-based and humanistic Modern period after about 1680 people's thoughts turned more to the problem of pain and suffering: in a law-governed world created by a supposedly benevolent Designer-God, why is there so much suffering? And how far can we diminish the amount of suffering in the world by developing and introducing better technologies, and better political arrangements?

Today, the argument has moved on again. People seem to remain as capable as ever of incomprehensibly wicked behaviour, but describing such behaviour as sinful or evil and seeking religious remedies for it does not seem quite so useful as formerly it did. As for the problem of suffering, we have learnt that a great deal can be done to diminish it by modern medicine, by applied science, and by competent social administration. Already most people can expect to live a full span of life, with much more varied company and wider cultural provision than our ancestors could ever have hoped for. To quite a large extent, we *can* make things better for ourselves and have already done so.

However, as everyone knows, there is no immediate prospect of our being altogether freed either from the shadow of sudden personal disaster or from the certainty of our own eternal death, and my present argument is simply that the extraordinary technical and political advances of the twentieth century have for many or most people shifted the spotlight away from moral and physical evil, and towards metaphysical evil.

Everything is utterly contingent; everything passes away, and I will soon pass away. So how am I to avoid sinking into the pessimism of the very long line of male literary curmudgeons who began with Schopenhauer and are now numberless?

Several answers are given. A very common one, given by Nietzsche, is that we must say a wholehearted Yes to life now, in the present moment. We cannot now hope to make our present life bearable by appealing to some Higher World or promised future in which everything will be put right, but it *is* possible to feel in the present moment that one is happy, and that our life is worthwhile. There are many familiar literary examples of this sentiment – for example in Browning, and in Henry James.

A second and somewhat subtler argument aims to show us that our feelings of discontent are irrational. It says: Things are what they are. *Outsidelessly*, we are humans in our human world, a world of signs in motion, and therefore of change. Very well: everything is *empty*, in the Buddhist sense. Everything is secondary, everything is transient – but how do you suppose things could really be otherwise? In an eternal and perfect world there could be no persons and no life. Think about human life: it is often messy and prickly and it is always death-haunted, but you would rather have it than not, wouldn't you? Therefore, as the Bible says: 'Choose life!'[2]

A third argument runs as follows: most of our gloomy thoughts about transience depend upon a contrast between *ourselves*, thought of as stable and self-identical beings, and *time*, as a power distinct from ourselves that threatens us.

For example, time may be seen as a rushing railway train or coach that hurtles along carrying us aboard it, and that will at some future moment crash and kill us all. Or time may be seen as eroding us and wearing us away by its constant attrition. Or we may picture ourselves as all sitting in a huge waiting-room. Now and again a name is called out, and one of us is led away, never to be seen again.[3] And so it has always been: every one of us will eventually be called and must disappear into the unknown; but we have no idea of who will be next, nor of what to expect.

And so it goes on: the three illustrations I have just given could be multiplied indefinitely by anyone with a good knowledge of literature – and especially of poetry. But they all depend upon thinking of time as extrinsic, other than ourselves, and as a threat.

---

2 Deuteronomy 30.19, etc.

3 A story from Pascal's *Pensées*.

But twenty years ago Dogen taught me to think: 'Wait a minute. I *am* the time of my life.[4] I *am* my own be-ing. I *myself* am slipping away at exactly the same speed as everything else.' And that gave me a sudden thought of eternity-in-the-midst-of-time. A similar effect can be produced by the old illustration of Einstein's treatment of time; for suppose that you are riding on a beam of light that is travelling away from a clock-face. Look back – and time is standing still!

Stories like these help to make a general point: the more I can learn to see *myself* as be-ing just the moving process of my own life, so that I really am completely embedded in and coincident with my own temporality, the closer I get to a consoling intuition of eternity in the midst of utter transience. People's fear of time and death is a fear of being *left out*. But I'm not being left out. I am always in the midst of It All.

All three of the types of argument that have been quoted have some value, and the third in particular has stayed with me. From time to time in the past I have used 'the Fountain' as a symbol of it. Every bit of the fountain is nothing but rushing formless transience: but now stand back from it a while, and see how it becomes still and consoling, a symbol of healing, refreshment, calm, and life's endless self-renewal.

Thus it appears that today, fully as much as in any earlier period, the contemplation of a great unifying religious symbol may give rise to intense religious comfort and happiness.

---

4 See Joan Stambaugh, *Impermanence is Buddha-Nature: Dogen's Understanding of Temporality*, Honolulu: University of Hawaii, 1990.

2

The Religious Symbol

Throughout Christianity's second millennium the Madonna and Child was easily the most popular subject in Christian art. It is said to be the topic of almost one-tenth of all the surviving religious paintings of the great Italian School. But perhaps the most highly venerated of all such works is the Virgin of Vladimir, an early Russian icon in the Byzantine style that now hangs – rather incongruously – in the Tretyakov Gallery, Moscow.[5] It is one of a group of rather similar icons, some of them now very blackened and much-repainted.

In these beautiful works the Virgin's face is large, looming, very thoughtful and loving, and intensely sad. Her beloved Child nuzzles close to her cheek, innocently happy in her love, because he is too young to know yet what she already knows about how his life will end.

Gazing at an icon of this kind has given religious consolation to thousands, perhaps millions, of ordinary Russians for about a thousand years. The Mary at whose face one gazes is the eternal Mother: she is not only the Mother of God, she is also Rachel weeping for her children, she is Mother Russia herself, she is 'the masses', the anonymous enduring common people, and she is one's own mother. Standing through the Liturgy for two or three hours every Sunday morning, the peasants are sustained by the vision of a love that eternally understands, suffers and still loves; for this painting of a woman's face is also a vision of Eternity. It's a vision of eternity that is a little too deeply nationalist and

---

5 See G. H. Hamilton, *The Art and Architecture of Russia* (The Pelican History of Art), Harmondsworth: Penguin Books, 1954, pp. 70f. and PL.32.

quietistic for me to share, but it is impossible not to be moved by it. The unifying and reconciling power of this symbol has helped a whole nation to endure some very cold and hard centuries. It has made their life bearable.

What makes a religious symbol such as the Virgin of Vladimir so powerful? Freud held that the relation between a mother and her male child is the most perfect of all human relationships, and also the perfect natural symbol of human solidarity and the continuity of the race. Auguste Comte planned to preserve this image above all others in his 'religion of humanity', and understandably so, for what other image could so comprehensively fuse together morality with nature, the most intense love with the earthiest biological factuality, and the individual human with common humanity? But to point this out is to see that a great religious icon does not merely *confirm* the old platonic binary oppositions (flesh and spirit, time and eternity, humanity and divinity, the individual and the universal, and so forth). On the contrary, it *synthesizes* them. All of them, to such a degree that it makes the Nietzschean description of Orthodox (and Catholic) worship as 'Platonism for the masses' look a good deal too crude. In fact, it would be better to say that the reconciled and blissful Unity into which the Liturgy and the Iconostasis lead the Orthodox peasant is 'beyond God'; or at least, beyond the God of standard metaphysical theism.

Why? Because in the standard philosophy of God there has to be an unbridgeable gulf between the world and God. The world has to be utterly dependent upon God, and God has to be absolutely independent and self-existent. Thus there is an infinite difference between the created and the Creator, and the same is true in standard theology. The gap between ourselves and God is so wide that God is quite unknown to us and unthinkable by us. Our only way to eternal happiness is by faith in the power and efficacy of the system of mediation, the bridge between ourselves and God, which is offered to us in the Christian revelation. We cannot see the bridge reaching all the way to the other side, but faith is to trust that it does so in the end. And the bridge is Christ, who himself is mediated to us by the Bible, the Church, the clergy and so on.

This official religious ideology was of course drawn up by the professional clergy, and therefore lays great emphasis upon their indispensability. They want to tell us that there are no short cuts: we cannot bypass the Church, the clergy and the sacraments. But the official ideology perhaps never appealed very greatly to any but the clergy themselves. Ordinary lay believers and mystics at prayer have always been content with the feeling of religious release and happiness that they get when for a while they step out of ordinary life and contemplate images of patient and enduring *human* love and suffering.

So it is then that, although official religious orthodoxy is always sharply dualistic and disciplinary, the way religious symbols work and the way mystics write tends always to blur the orthodox distinctions and lead us beyond them into undifferentiated, Empty[6] and timeless bliss.

Against this background I can now explain the use to be made of the symbol of the Fountain in the present essay. I have already argued that in the late Modern and Postmodern periods we have become acutely aware of the Empty transience of all existence and of ourselves. We have lost the old belief in a timeless Real World beyond the world of everyday appearances, and it is now very common for people to suffer from severe time-dread and fear of death. For such people, the Fountain may be an efficacious religious symbol. It is nothing but a formless rush of events, pouring out and passing away continuously: but when it is seen from a distance it becomes still, and appears as a soothing symbol of life, healing and repose. So much is this so that in many parts of the world a fountain is the central design feature both of a city

---

6 When I use the word Empty with a capital E, I intend the Buddhist meaning of the word: 'Empty of own-being', insubstantial.

square, and of a paradise-garden, whether it be a cemetery or a pleasure-garden.

There is a further, and very great, attraction: the Fountain is a symbol that unexpectedly offers us the chance to reconnect Cosmos and Ethos, Nature and Morality, the way the world goes and the way we would do best to live. Since Newton and Darwin it has been common to experience a sharp split between Is and Ought, between (in Plato's jargon) Physics and Ethics. The scientific picture of the world is usually said to be completely mechanistic and non-moral. The Universe is very *cold*, and we cannot look to it for any sort of human warmth, moral guidance and support. It is utterly indifferent to us. But I am suggesting that the Fountain-image can heal this fundamental split in modern culture. It can teach us as individual moral agents to live generously, by pouring ourselves out continuously into expression. We should go with the flow of life. We should try to live purely affirmatively, without any recoiling or revulsion or other 'reactive' or negative emotions. We should totally reject the popular spirituality of introversion, by which we spend much of our lives recollecting ourselves, looking within, and seeking to purify our own supposedly immortal souls. I have no soul: I am not a substance, and there is no real me. There is only what I am able, rather uncertainly, to make of myself as I go along, and what you can make of me: that is, I am only a stream of events, a process in time, and all ideas of me are only interpretations of that process, or bits of it.

From this I conclude that we should live by self-giving love. We should live generously. We should live hard. We should burn. And if we live by self-outing, pouring ourselves out and passing away all the time, then we will be living a 'dying life' and our death will be the crown of life, its last work and not merely its abrupt and violent cessation.

The range of themes that are all drawn together in the Fountain-image is, as we shall see, very wide. Two further explanatory comments need to be made.

First, in the Bible the developed, gravity-powered ornamental fountain seems not to appear. In hot Middle-Eastern countries a fountain is a fount, or font, or wellspring, or simply a freshwater spring that comes bubbling up out of the ground. It's 'the water of life', and an oasis or a garden may develop around it. The gravity-powered fountain was developed by the Arabs and the Persians, and becomes prominent in Renaissance Europe. The pumped fountain that springs high like a geyser, and then spreads out like an umbrella as it falls back into its bowl cannot (I suppose) be more than two centuries old. It became a familiar feature of public parks in the great nineteenth-century cities. But it is of importance to me, because if there is a way of imagining a fountain which continually recycles its own waters, then it may open up the idea of the Eternal Return. As the waters fall back, they may recoup the energy that initially propelled them upwards. Thus the Fountain may come to be thought of as perpetually recycling its own waters, and a spectator of it will see a world made of nothing but a fleeting stream of contingent events, but which as a whole, and seen from outside, is a timeless, blissful totality. At times in the past, and especially in the 1990s, I have been so haunted by this idea that I have summed up my whole philosophy under the label 'Energetic Spinozism'.[7]

The second promised supplementary comment concerns alternatives to the Fountain as a unifying religious symbol. The most important of these is the Sun, with its associated ideas of fire and a lamp. This image came to me very strongly in 1994:

We should live as the Sun does. The process by which it lives and the process by which it dies are one and the same. It hasn't a care. It simply expends itself gloriously, and in so doing gives life to us all.[8]

---

7 Or the Torus. See my *After All*, London: SCM Press, 1994, pp. 57–61.
8 *Ibid.*, p. 109.

Like the Fountain, the Sun is also energetic, outpouring, self-emptying process. It too may be used in order to reconnect ethics with cosmology, and it is of course also a long-established religious symbol. I pursued the image, and went straight on from the words quoted above to the writing of *Solar Ethics* (1995). The images of fire and of a lamp that radiates illumination can scarcely be avoided in this present discussion. But for reasons that will become apparent, it is the Fountain that will occupy the central position on this occasion. And notice, by the way, that in garden design the Fountain is always placed at a *focal* point, where many paths meet.

3

The Fountain: Be-ing

In a deservedly famous brief discussion, Aristotle points out the large number of different senses in which a person may be said to 'have' something. Similarly, there is a very large number of distinct senses in which it may be claimed that something is 'in being', 'exists', or is 'real' or 'extant'. So large, that we can quickly confound all those straightforward, down-to-earth people who feel quite sure that they know how to draw a clear line between what's real and what isn't, by asking them about various social institutions and conventions. Is Beethoven's Fourth Piano Concerto a 'real' thing? What sort of object is it? Point it out to me, please! And where does it lurk between performances of it? Alternatively, since they are apt to describe anyone who is very keen on money as 'materialistic', try asking them what money is in these days when it is no longer just gold, nor paper, and we are rapidly moving into a fully computerized and cashless economy. It's 'really' quite surprisingly difficult to say clearly just what money is now, and similar difficulties are becoming very widespread as the virtual worlds of the media and of cyberspace get bigger and bigger, and more and more deeply interwoven with the world of everyday life. Computer geeks notoriously can begin to confuse the virtual and the 'real'. Perhaps this is a new version of what happened at the time of the Industrial Revolution, when people became acutely aware of a cultural rift, and learnt to cope with it by making a broad distinction between two great worlds: there was the hard, masculine, public world of our competitive, science-based industrial society, and there was the more feminine world of private life, of morality, religion and the creative im- agination. The Victorians tried to keep these two worlds rather sharply distinct. But today the real and the fictional are already, or are fast becoming, thoroughly interwoven everywhere.

Aware of the growing difficulty, Wittgenstein argued for pluralism. Take the case of goodness. When I'm buying a lawn-mower, I am pretty clear in my mind about the criteria for something's being a *good lawnmower*, and when I'm asked whether I have had a *good holiday*, I know again pretty well what sort of things my friend is asking about. But in more general contexts things get vaguer. What could absolute, context-neutral, universal goodness *be*? There are traditional answers, such as 'the unity of all the compossible perfections; that is, of all the (compatible) qualities that it's better to have than not to have' – but this is getting hopelessly woolly, and we begin to suspect that we are wasting our time. 'Absolute' goodness, of no specific kind, is too vague an idea to be useful for any particular purpose. Similarly with existence. In a mathematical context, one can ask if there exists any prime number between 21 and 24; and in a literary context one can ask if David Copperfield had any brothers or sisters. In a scientific context one may say that something such as 'the force of gravity' that certainly 'exists' under Newton's theory is not at all the same in modern physics, where there are various possibilities of reducing it to an effect of the curvature of space, or even of arguing about gravitational waves or particles. How much 'reality' something has may look very different in different theoretical contexts. Still more difficult and controversial are disputes about the 'objectivity' of morals, or of mathematical truth. So Wittgenstein suggests that we can with no difficulty talk about existence within the context of particular fields of discourse and language-games. But we should avoid 'the absolute-existence mistake' – that is, the error of supposing that there is any general or absolute is-ness that all existing things have in common, or in which all things in existence are Grounded; and we should not attempt to draw a clear and agreed line around all the various things that *do really exist*, in order to separate them from all the imaginary, postulated and conventional things that *don't really exist*. It's a mistake to feel that you need to, or indeed *can*, draw such a line. So we should accept a certain pluralism about existence.

Wittgenstein's point of view marks a big advance upon the old metaphysical ideas about existence and the Real that we inherited from Plato and Aristotle. It is also a big advance upon the crude scientific realism we have inherited from Descartes, which feels the need to assert the existence of an objectively real and ready-made world out there, of which our current scientific theory is (we are to suppose) a true and accurate copy – or at least, diagram. That kind of scientific realism is open to many objections, two of which are that scientific theory is in continual – and sometimes fundamental – change, and second, that in scientific reporting the observer, though always presupposed, is always systematically ex-cluded and 'left unthought'. Science seems always to need to conceal from itself its own human, cultural and linguistic 'situatedness'.

There are then good reasons for questioning popular scientific realism. But nor should we be content to accept Wittgenstein's kind of linguistic naturalism, or positivism. He will say only that 'This language-game is played' – which is surely much *too* pluralistic and passive. It sounds too like the position of someone who is becoming tired and pessimistic, and will soon be giving up philosophy.

So I take a slightly different view. Like life, language has no outside. Language goes everywhere, and there are some things that are true of language everywhere. If so, language is philosophy's base, and we may say that something exists if it's a worthwhile topic of discourse, if it's debatable, and if sense is talked about it. So the whole field of existence, the world, is co-extensive with the endless, ongoing conversation of humanity. Language in motion = 'Life' = the going-on of things in the human life-world = 'the Fray' = Be-ing. Within that vast hum of communication – the Web, the noosphere, cyberspace – we are all busy arguing with each other about our valuations, our theories, our proposals for improvement, and generally about what's worth taking more seriously than what. But it's all 'life'; it's all Be-ing. And within this ceaseless motion of our language we are all the time constructing and renegotiating our various worlds and fields of discourse. What exists is what is linguistically alive, and truth is the current consensus in a particular field.

But if the whole world of existence is getting to look more and more like a huge communications network, a worldwide web, then it is indeed like a fountain, for it is streaming out and scattering all the time. And this stream of signs needs a *body* that it forms and in turn is given substance by: it needs a river of outpouring *energies* to ride upon and to modulate. Where does it *spring* from? What motivates it?

Here we come up against the limits of language. The whole world of language out in expression, in motion, is what I am calling the world of Be-ing, temporal existence. But where does the outpouring and scattering motion of the world *spring* from? What's the source – or mouth, or vent – from which it is silently pouring out?

The Western tradition is divided at this point. The dominant tradition of theism grounds the world upon the action of a creative masculine Will that posits *fully formed* created be-ing and then maintains it in be-ing from moment to moment. The imagery is dry and sharp-edged, whereas in the other and more feminine tradition the stuff of the world is like a still-unformed liquid that flows out from a feminine Void, *khora*, or womb. The words *mater, material, matrix* are invoked, and I am among those who may claim to have coined the term *M/Other* for it. Here the world-stuff, as it strives to get out into expression, is no more than a jostling, foaming tumult of formless possibility, or white noise. Then language closes down on it, fixes it, forms it – and is carried away by it.

On this second account, non-language – the formless, ineffable unthing from which the world of be-ing flows out – is Being, crossed out. It is the O, the mouth of the womb, the E-vent, or the vessel from which living water flows. In some early writings I inclined to identify the stream of outflowing energy upon which language rides as *libido*, or *life*. Today I prefer a more agnostic account: that from which the fully formed world of language-in-motion issues is our M/Other. It is dark, it is unknown, it is (symbolically) female. It is Being, crossed out, because it is extra-verbal. It is the Jewish mystical *Ein Sof*. But being language's Other it remains dark and awesome, and no more can be said about it. No more *should* be said of it.

You may already have discovered that – like me – you enjoy attempting a dark, wordless, silent meditation upon the Void, our M/Other. If you would like to try it but find it difficult, try an Abstract Expressionist painting such as one of the last works of Mark Rothko or of Ad Reinhardt, to get you started. Their works are just black fields. If that is still too difficult, try the very concrete but entirely correct and appropriate imagery of a painting such as *La Source* (1856) by J.-A.-D. Ingres, in the Musée d'Orsay at Paris.

There may be an objection to my imagery, in that it dates from a prescientific and sexist period when Matter and Form were 'the Mother and Father of Being'.[9] But the old imagery is extra-ordinarily tenacious, and my citation of it is not intended to be sexist. We all of us, females as well as males, issue from the same symbolically female prelinguistic Darkness (the Chaos-monster of myth), and the meeting of language and non-language which gives rise to a streaming, formed and illuminated world of Be-ing takes place in all of us. Listen tonight to the running of language in your own head. It's all there, and is the same for you whether you yourself happen to be male or female.

---

9 Plato's phrase.

4

The Fountain: Language

Natural motions such as those associated with wind, or water, or fire seem to fascinate us, and we are ready to watch them by the hour. They symbolize transience, but they are usually calming and peaceful to contemplate. I well remember how hypnotized I was when as a boy of 15 I first saw Brownian motion under a microscope. There are also some motions that everyone has noticed, but which have almost never been discussed. One of them can be seen now if you will shut your eyes firmly, put your palms over them, and patiently study your visual field. It is minutely speckled with various pinpricks of colour against a dark background. Floating patches of greenish-yellow linger for a while, and then fade and are replaced by royal blue and other darker colours. The whole gives an impression of foaming, sparkling, flickering, surging motion in a space that is not quite regular and Euclidean, but rather unstable and distorted. Evidently when the retina is in darkness it does not lie quite passive and inert. On the contrary, after-images linger upon it and little waves of sensation float across it. The cells on the retina are hair-trigger sensitive: they *prickle*. There is no absolute darkness, just as in modern physics there is no absolute void or nothingness. Even in empty space at absolute zero temperature, there is a faint quantum foam of particles briefly popping into and out of existence. So it is with the eye, and also with the ear, where a faint fizz and crackle of white noise can be heard by the sensitive even in what might be considered 'dead' silence. Have you ever been silent enough to hear your own pulsing blood?

The same principle applies to the brain. Except under heavy general anaesthetic, there is always at least a low level of brain activity, and therefore of consciousness.[10] I have reached the age at which one no longer sleeps deeply, and so perforce spend much time at night dozily listening to the language-generating area of the brain fountaining out a stream of words, associations and diverging trains of thought (that is part-sentences). It is a torrential mixture of sense and nonsense, pouring out and scattering at speed. Such is thought: scattering language.

I'm scatty. I was brought up to suppose that men's thinking is typically convergent, whereas women's thinking is typically divergent. By an effort of will a man concentrates his whole attention and sticks to the point as he traces a single line of argument, the straight and narrow path of reason. Whereas a woman – well, she is thought to be continually distracted by sidelines, associations, memories and speculations, not to mention the well-known fact that there are always numerous other matters that she has to bear in mind all the time, such as whether her children are adequately shod, fed and safe. As Henry Tilney remarks gallantly:

> Miss Morland, no one can think more highly of the understanding of women than I do. In my opinion, nature has given them so much that they never find it necessary to use more than half.

But the time for such jocularity is now past, for during the twentieth century we gradually came to see that all thinking is a confused rushing motion of words or other signs – an incompletely executed soliloquy, 'inner speech' in our heads; and secondly, that language (Greek, *glōtta*, *glōssa*, Latin, *lingua*: the unstoppable tongue) is thoroughly feminine in both sexes. Listen to your own head at night, male reader. You will hear bubbling, burbling, babble, babel – language pouring out, sly, punning, easily deflected and distracted, diverging and scattering.[11] That's

---

10 Hence, surely, Descartes's conviction that the soul 'always thinks'.

11 Jacques Lacan recognized that the Unconscious 'thinks in language', because it notices puns. This has helped later thinkers to recognize that all thought is a motion of language.

why I said that I am scatty, for the cultural ideal of masculine *logos* represented an attempt by humans to persuade themselves that by an effort of will they could achieve something like divine command over their own process of expression. Meaning itself could be firmly pinned down, so that what my words mean is kept in exact co-incidence with what I intend, what *I* 'mean' to say.

This profoundly 'theological' idea that linguistic meaning can be controlled by the will of a sufficiently self-possessed, iron-willed and masculine speaker is still further confirmed in English by the use of the same verb 'mean' in a *causal* sense ('those dark clouds mean that it will soon rain'). Throw in the popular belief that the 'real' meaning of a word can be found by looking up its etymology, its original, founding, and supposedly normative meaning, and one begins to understand how pervasively theological our culture formerly was. Undisciplined, wayward speech is frightening. We mustn't allow our tongues to run away with us: hence the traditionally popular sermon topic of 'the government of the tongue'. What is needed to keep language and the world in order is the rule of one original founding and commanding Will that has complete control of language and therefore of all the world. Whereas inconsequential talkativeness equals lack of control, an untidy world.

So people used to think, especially in the days when much of education was concerned with teaching the young dead languages that can be relied upon to keep conveniently still, and standard texts of which there were socially approved and well-established interpretations. In those social conditions it was easy to fail to notice the extraordinary *shiftiness* of language. Words run, and meaning proliferates. I cannot hope fully to control the meaning of what I have said. There is no way of guarding it against any possibility of future misinterpretation. And in fact I am acutely aware that many things that I wrote decades ago have changed since I published them. Cultural conditions have changed, language itself has changed, and I have changed – and I do not know how it is that some people's texts have the capacity to keep renewing themselves by taking on interesting new meanings as the years go by, whereas other people's texts become stale and boring.

To return to my scattiness, how is it that the language-generating area of the brain churns out all the time such a complex, disorderly, manifold stream of words? We still find it hard to improve on the old Schopenhauer-and-Freud model. Our consciousness, such as it is, floats upon a complex, outpouring torrent of mixed biological feelings that seek gratification, or at least symbolic expression. All the words of our language have feelings and valuations *currently* associated with them, so that as my biological feeling struggles to come out into expression, even while I am lying in bed in the darkness, it naturally jumps at once into the verbal signs or chains of signs that are nearest to hand and most readily give it the outlet it seeks.

All this implies that 'thought' runs almost as quickly as a computer. Brainwaves spread rapidly over the cortex. The language-generator riffles through its own database very fast, and the emotional drive that seeks expression moves equally quickly to snatch at and assume the verbal form that most nearly suits it. But then, as all words are linked by many different paths of association with other words, one thing quickly leads to another. Verbal trains begin to radiate away in several directions at once. At night, relatively relaxed, I can follow a good deal of this, but during the day so much is happening so fast that I cannot keep track of it all. I have tried carrying a small notebook as poets do, in order to jot down immediately anything good that comes into my head, but on the whole the night is the best period. Quiet gardening, on one's knees weeding the vegetable patch, can with luck also provide the right conditions for 'thinking'. The disorderly wandering of the mind is the seedbed of thought.

Thinking? It cannot be done by a concentrated effort of the will. By that means one can produce only headings, 'bullet points', diagrams, summaries, analyses and the like. Rationales. Interesting *novelty* can be obtained only by briefly reviewing the problem with which one is concerned – turning it over in one's mind, as the phrase goes – and then one must hand it over to the language-generator, relax, doze off, and wait to see what comes up. Like I said, I'm scatty. Being scatty is the way to think. We should be accustomed by now to the idea that complex patterns of order can arise out of the free play of a variety of forces, a mixture of chance and necessity, disorder and order, regularity and serendipity. In a mechanistic Newtonian universe there is not much likelihood of any very interesting novelty ever arising. But the somewhat disorderly world of modern genetics has proved fabulously creative, and the fountain of language in our heads can give birth to great riches if we learn how to let it run most freely and productively. Trust the Fountain!

5

The Fountain: Big-Bang Cosmology

As early as the 1920s the American astronomer Edwin Hubble established that there are many other galaxies in the Universe beyond our own 'Milky Way', and that these other galaxies are approximately uniformly distributed. Furthermore, he was able by spectography to show that the Universe is expanding uniformly and very rapidly. Since then we have not doubted that we live in a vast expanding Universe, but it was not until after much debate that in the 1970s the 'Big Bang' cosmology at last came to be generally accepted. Even yet there are still many loose ends, but we seem now to be agreed that the Universe is best described as an enormous explosion, originating at a point commonly described as the 'initial singularity', and still spreading. Very soon after the beginning, a range of chemical elements began to form, and in time, as stars, planetary systems and comets developed, structures of great interest, beauty and complexity appeared – notably in our own planetary system. But it seems that in the very long run all matter will decay into radiation. Finally, there will be only a faint tingle of radiation in an immeasurably vast void, though it remains possible that the cosmos will turn out to be cyclical. In which case the present explosion will be followed by an implosion that will return everything back into the origin.

The Universe, it seems, is just one great Event (or pulse), a vast explosion of energy still slowly scattering and dying. It is not, as they say, 'going anywhere'; it's going everywhere, and its history does not fulfil any purpose. It happens to have given rise to us, and we happen to have a great deal of time left yet, provided that we do not rashly extinguish ourselves; but eventually we will disappear without trace.

Such is the human situation, according to the best knowledge available to us. How do we react, how *should* we react, to this new and perhaps chilly vision of our condition and our prospects?

Some indication of the range of possible reactions has already been given during the earlier history of modern astronomy. In 1543 Nicholas Copernicus had published his work *On the Revolutions of the Heavenly Bodies*, which broke with the traditional Earth-centred, and indeed Man-centred, cosmology implied by standard church doctrine. His ideas were taken up by the errant Dominican friar Giordano Bruno, who admired the beauty of Copernicus' vision of the cosmos and developed it into a kind of pantheism that foreshadows the thought of Spinoza. He was burnt for heresy at Rome in 1600.

Half a century later, Blaise Pascal contemplated the machine-Universe of Galileo and Descartes, and found it very chilling for someone who had hoped to see in the sky the populous Heaven of religion. 'The eternal silence of those infinite spaces terrifies me.' Pascal withdrew into an internalized religion of the heart – a reaction repeated after Newton in the rise of Pietism on the European mainland, and of Methodism in Britain. 'Natural religion' faded, and the emphasis began to fall upon faith, and upon eternal salvation after death.

The reaction after Newton was particularly interesting in the field of ethics. Reading Newton's *Principia*, you could perhaps admire the elegant design of the world machine, but you could no longer draw moral inferences from nature. The world might still be thought of as revealing the divine power and wisdom, but the way it ran did not in any way reveal the divine *goodness*. Nor did it fulfil any purpose or evince any special care for us. All ideas of miracles and of particular providences began to decline. A few writers of the rationalist school attempted to ground the ethical in pure reason and ideas of rational self-consistency, but the more interesting ethical response in Britain was the beginning of modern humanitarianism. From now on, humans are apparently alone. Ethics is only human, and we must ground the ethical in our own reciprocal benevolence, sympathy and fellow-feeling. In a very cold Universe, we must love one another or die. Auden, remember, corrected this last line to '*and* die'.

What, then, about today? How is our own thinking in philosophy, religion and ethics responding to the new cosmology that now seems pretty securely established?

In the first place, we note a worldwide neo-conservative and often anti-scientific religious reaction, which is often described as 'fundamentalism'. Historically, it began as a reaction against Darwinism, biblical criticism and liberal theology, especially in North America at the end of the nineteenth century. But today it is much more consciously a counter-cultural revolt against what it sees as the 'meaninglessness', 'lack of purpose', and moral scepticism of modern Western secular culture. That is, Darwin is no longer the only nor even the chief enemy. Our entire scientific-industrial culture and world-view has come to be seen as morally and spiritually empty, and indeed terrifying.

Others however will react more as Spinoza did to the Universe of Descartes. They will say that we clearly do need to give up the picture of the cosmos as being a kind of superstate ruled by a transcendent King of Kings, who has built into his realm a natural moral law and into us an organ of moral knowledge (in effect, conscience *plus* 'synderesis') which recognizes its binding authority. It is time, then, for all of us to give up seeing the world in terms of almighty Power and the universal rule of the moral Law. Instead we should lay the emphasis upon our own immersion in Nature, upon its briefly flowering beauty, and upon our own continuity with it. Calvinist businessmen merely ravaged Nature, but our own more up-to-date and science-based vision of the world may lead us – indeed *has* led us – in the direction of environmentalism. We are immersed in Nature, and should love it, not just rule it. Along similar lines, in the 1990s I would often describe my own philosophy as a form of 'energetic Spinozism'. I wanted to go with the flow, and to love all life as long as I'm part of it. As for the new cosmology, it indeed fails to give us any cosily human consolation; but I can and do find it spectacular and exhilarating.

So far I have been suggesting that our reaction to the new cosmology continues and develops lines of thought that were already appearing in response to the beginning of modern astronomy in the sixteenth and seventeenth centuries. But there is more to tell yet. I suggest that we can already make out the beginnings of a sharp turn towards *emotivism* and *expressivism*.

The main old-Western tradition combined Plato's philosophy with Christian spirituality. It praised at least partial detachment from the world of immediate sense-experience and the emotions, and instead gave the highest value to sovereign Reason, long-termism, and the rational contemplation (*theōria*) of eternal verities. One should 'look up' to a Higher World above in which one hoped to find one's last home. In every sphere, theory ranked higher than practice. When people who came out of this kind of background took up moral philosophy or philosophy of art, their chief concern was with trying to demonstrate that our moral judgements or our aesthetic judgements were rational – that is, 'objective'. One tried to demonstrate that something out there makes one's moral judgements or one's judgements about artistic quality *true*. Quasi-factually true, out-there true, theoretically or 'speculatively' true, platonically true: and on such debates British moral philosophy in the twentieth century wasted far too much effort. As for the view that morality is just human and is grounded in human feeling, it was described as 'emotivism', associated in particular with C. L. Stevenson, and deplored. Poor old Stevenson[12] was a Dreadful Warning: his were the conclusions you must not reach.

Thus the dominant styles both in philosophy and in theology,

---

12 C. L. Stevenson, *Ethics and Language*, New Haven: Yale University Press, 1944; 'The Emotive Meaning of Ethical Terms', *Mind* 46, pp. 14–31. Interest in emotivism has been revived recently by Jesse J. Prinz, *The Emotional Construction of Morals*, Oxford and New York: Oxford University Press, 2007. See also Ole Riis and Linda Woodhead, *A Sociology of Religious Emotion*, Oxford and New York: Oxford University Press, 2010.

and both in ethics and spirituality, tended to devalue everything to do with the senses and the emotions, and everything immediate and transient. Spirituality was introvertive and otherworldly. One withdrew one's attention from this world of the senses and of temptation, and instead looked up to the world of eternal truth that is the true home of Reason. And from Plato to Kant the philosophers were unmarried, just like the monks and many or all of the secular clergy.

When did it all begin to change? There was an old principle in philosophy that reason by itself does not *move* anything, and during the eighteenth century a revaluation of the life of feeling comes through at many levels: in the ethics of human fellow-feeling, the sentiment of benevolence; in the early Evangelical Revival with its high valuation of religious feeling and a changed life; and even in David Hume's recognition that reason has to be the slave of the passions. By the end of the century the Romantic Movement is becoming intensely emotive-expressive, and soon the names are coming thick and fast: Wordsworth, Darwin, Nietzsche, Freud, Lawrence and far too many others to name here. The emergent common theme is that we are of course animals, products of Nature. As in Schopenhauer's philosophy the Will comes out into Representation, so all our life is a continuous welling-up and flowing-out of emotion into either direct, or at least displaced, or symbolic expression. One should seek to live as affirmatively as possible, to live by the heart. Instead of wasting our lives in saving ourselves for an imaginary next life, we should commit ourselves to living *this* life to the full while we have it. So we reject the spirituality of introversion and self-purification, and embrace instead a new ethic and spirituality of extraversion and expression, living hard, spending ourselves. Instead of retiring into semi-darkness and seclusion, we should 'come out', in every sense, and put on a brave show.

In all the most-developed human cultures the human being is always a microcosm, a little world, a small counterpart of the great world, the Macrocosm. Today, outgoing, affirmative, extravertive, *solar* living is the human being's Big-Bang *micro*cosmology. Everything explodes into being, radiates, pours out and passes away – and we too should live like that, *generously*. Since we now have no further world to expect beyond this one, and even this one is passing away rapidly, we should spend ourselves completely and be quite content in due course to pass away and be forgotten along with everything else. Life's a package deal: it cannot be re-negotiated, and there is no alternative. So we should buy into it, and make the very most of it.

6

The Fountain: Living Waters

Since antiquity, men have been symbolically associated with the elements of air and fire. Their bodies are more fully formed, angular and with a more-nearly continuous boundary, so that a man much more than a woman sees himself as a relatively isolated individual, more exposed to danger, expendable, and above all, mortal.

Women were associated with the elements of earth and water.[13] Their bodies are more rounded and less fully formed, and are damper and leakier. Through her body a woman is woven physically into a line of generations. A matriliny, for example, feels like an interlocked chain of bodies, each of which opens below to release the next one down the line. There was – at least from Hebrews to Leibniz – a parallel suggestion to the effect that future generations are similarly boxed, one inside another, within the testes of a man. It was called the theory of *emboîtement*,[14] but it never carried quite the same symbolic power as the woman's sense that her body is a physical link, interlocked with other links, in the chain of life. She is not just a single life: life has flowed through her in a way that not even death can take away from her, so that a woman is on the whole much less haunted by personal horror of mortality, as final, complete exclusion, than a man is. *Her* life feels more like *universal* life, the life that goes on.

In recent English literature, with the final disappearance for most people of religious belief and with it of any idea of life after

---

13 As ever, I recommend Aristotle, *On the Generation of Animals* as a splendid, and often unintentionally funny, course in basic sexism.

14 The theory was taken up by Leibniz from the Dutch microscopists, and influenced his theory of 'monads'. For *emboîtement* in Hebrews, see Chapter 7.

death, horror of death among men has become very strong indeed.[15] Symbolically, it is almost as if man is Death and woman is Life. He looks to her for comfort on precisely that point – as if she is *his* Fountain – though it must be said that woman, for her part, suffers more from time-dread (anxiety about getting older and progressively losing her power over men) and also suffers more grief, especially over the deaths of her men. Perhaps in the end the accounting comes out fairly evenly balanced, though I for one suspect that on average woman does better than man. A man's life is the life of one mortal individual: a woman's life is the life of the whole species. So she lives longer. That's an unphilosophical thing to say, but you know there's truth in it.

Her final advantage is therefore that woman is on the whole more *cosmological* than man – that is, her body, and in particular her womb, has more world-building symbolic power. Here, I think, Freud underestimated woman when he made 'penis envy', so important, and any corresponding 'womb-envy' relatively unimportant. On the contrary, all Be-ing flows continuously from the womb of time, around the world furnaces and kilns are womb-shaped, reflecting the formation of metals in the womb of the earth, and woman's womb is an internal font containing the primal waters of creation. When 'her waters break' new life issues from her. Finally, within every church building the font is a womb of rebirth. So potent and pervasive is all this symbolism that it is hardly surprising that woman, and not man, was such a prom-inent subject of the earliest art. In order to establish patriarchy and our masculinist monotheism, it was long thought necessary to wage a cultural war against women which has left a persistent legacy of hostility and prejudice, but Gustav Courbet deserves respect for deliberately and plainly defying it in his painting entitled *The Creation of the World*.

Against this background we can raise the question of water-

---

15 I have in mind all the obvious names: Betjeman, Larkin, Amis *pére et fils* and Julian Barnes.

symbolism, and in particular the relation between water and life. According to some of the oldest and most familiar sayings in the whole history of Western philosophy, 'Everything flows', and 'You cannot step into the same river twice'. So why are rivers so *friendly*, and so easily personified – and as males, indeed? A river is an old man, a Father. Surely rivers ought to be perceived as unstable, lacking clear boundaries and without any principle of identity. Elsewhere, we have been citing the way a beck tumbling down a steep hillside looks from a mile away just like a glistening, motionless snailtrack. From a sufficient distance, waterfalls (and, indeed, fountains) appear still. Ponds and lakes can be very still, clear and deep, but rivers seem almost always to be in motion, and we actively appreciate their motion – their transience (literally, 'going by'). Why?

During a very hot dry summer I have seen the level of the Cam drop, and the river's motion become eventually imperceptible. Duckweed and filamentous algae spread. The river looks unpleasant, as if it is dying: and *there* is the clue. The motion of a river is a very powerful natural symbol of life and its perpetual self-renewal. Like the welling-up of a spring from the ground, the moving water of a river is *living* water, the water of life, a natural counterpart of the amniotic waters.

Notice, finally, that there are numerous and varied symbols of the religious consolation that we get from life's perpetual self-renewal. Dawn and the return of waking consciousness is one of them: 'New every morning is the Love / Our wakening and up-rising prove' is a good and vivid example. Another is the return every springtime of familiar and well-loved wild flowers, insects and migratory birds. 'O Pulchritudo! Tam antiqua, tam nova', says Augustine: O Beauty, so old and so new! Each spring, I wonder how many more times I shall rejoice in this familiar return: but there is also comfort in the thought that it will continue, for a while at least, when I am no longer around to see it. And *that* is a thought that we associate very strongly with our pleasure in the sight of our own grandchildren.

The basic fountain-idea, that endlessly self-renewing utter transience is very beautiful and religiously consoling, seems at first sight to be quite at variance with the main tradition of Western theistic-platonic metaphysics. But it was always *there* as a minority voice. In the Hebrew Bible/the 'Old Testament' there is a very strong tendency to treat ordinary biological life as divine, and even to treat the genitals as sacred.[16] And in later Christian language all three persons of the Trinity are strongly associated with life. In Meister Eckhart, arguably one of the two or three most brilliant individuals in the entire Christian tradition, there is a great deal which effectively equates 'God' with 'life'.[17]

---

16 For example Psalm 29.9, Genesis 24.2.
17 See my *Mysticism After Modernity*, Oxford: Blackwell, 1998.

7

The Fountain: The Human Self and its Drive to Expression

A human being is a fountain of signs. By the ways we behave in different social settings, by our body language, by the clothes we wear, and by the things we say we are all the time sending out messages, making statements, putting in our twopenn'orth, making our contribution, competing for attention, doing our thing, trying to join in even at the risk of getting the wrong end of the stick – the idioms are numberless, and they all say the same thing, which is that we are all of us intensely communicative animals. We are just burning to have our say.

All this is a cliché now, but it has only become so since the mid-twentieth century and the enormous late-modern expansion of the means of travel and communication. Everyone has gained access successively to rail travel, daily newspapers, the telephone, the motor car, television, air travel, popular music and magazines, and most recently mobile phones, text messaging, email, the internet and the World Wide Web. If we were not ultra-communicative before all this, then we certainly are now.

In addition, during the second half of the twentieth century popular books with titles like *The Presentation of Self in Everyday Life*, and *Games People Play* have successfully established the notion that in everyday life we are all of us actors, who play a variety of roles which we have learnt to keep distinct. Thus a child craftily adapts its speech and behaviour to the company it is in, whether in the playground or the classroom, at home or with grandparents. Film actors, politicians and others soon become very conscious of their 'public image', and get into the habit of acting up to it – for example, by always presenting themselves with a cigar, or a pipe, or a particular quiff of hair or style of necktie. Following them, we have gradually (and, in the case of many men, reluctantly) learnt to live in constant awareness of the impression we are making upon others. Nietzsche was I think the very first to voice the suspicion that there *is* no real self behind all our various assumed images, roles, masks. Just as there are no facts but only interpretations, interpretations all the way down, so he suggested that there is no real self or 'core' self, but only masks behind masks, all the way down. And this thoroughly postmodern insight ends the reality/appearance distinction and makes the world itself into a Big Bang of communication, a dance of signs. With which we reach the later thought of Jean Baudrillard.

Where did these ideas begin? With Schopenhauer. From Parmenides to Hegel, over some 23 centuries, the main Western tradition had assumed that if there is a World-Ground or Most-Real-Being at all, then it must be One, self-existent and perfect. But Schopenhauer was one of the many creative people who have inherited a burden of psychological pain and disharmony from parents in conflict with each other, or from a neglectful mother whose social life was too busy to leave her with time to love her child. In addition, I guess without any definite evidence, Schopenhauer can scarcely have failed to notice Paul's very striking lines in Romans 7 and 8 about his own psychological conflict, and about the whole of creation 'groaning in travail'. At any rate, Schopenhauer's atheism enabled him to recognize both in the Cosmos and within the human self a painfully divided noumenal Will struggling with itself and seeking some degree of relief by coming out into phenomenal representation (jargon for symbolic expression). Both in Nature and in the human soul, the *Sturm und Drang* of Romantic art are the norm. Everything struggles for expression and thereby for reconciliation with itself.

Out of this circle of ideas has come the main reason why we human beings are so compulsively, and indeed obsessively, communicative. We are seeking what Freud – a keen follower of

Schopenhauer – was to call the 'talking cure'. By coming out into symbolic expression we can to some extent purge and relieve our painful feelings and, still better, if we can find the right symbols we may even be able to reconcile them. By communicating my feeling, by expressing myself, I am thus able *both* to get it all off my chest *and* to get myself together. Coming out is therapeutic: gossip is redemption – and you will recall that a gossip is a godsib, someone who is close kin like a godparent, someone with whom you can talk really freely.

From this, we see that the human self, like a *dramatis persona*, is theatrical. We produce our own selfhood insofar as we are able to get ourselves together through our own self-expression, and in our dealings with other people. And I shouldn't need to point out that the self as I conceive it is always utterly transient. We are able to get ourselves together, to fiction a fairly unified selfhood that we present to others, only partially and always very briefly. As we 'pass away', indeed.

Should one be miserable about one's own utter transience? No: what is making so many people miserable is their own thoroughly confused attachment to the idea of an eternal world of perfect bliss in which nothing will ever change – a dream rather like the timeless rural idyll that has long attracted urbanized Europeans. In fact, as soon as industrialism developed in Europe country folk were only too glad to leave 'the countryside' and get into the cities as fast as they could. Given the chance, people will always prefer the city, history and social change to the old rural serfdom. Of course they will: timelessness is neither more nor less than death. We cannot even conceive personal life except as temporal, and if I reflect I find that all the beauties I love most are transient, *and* that it is precisely for their transience that I love them. I cannot coherently wish them to be anything but transient, and the same goes for myself.

Notice also one or two interesting consequences of our move to an urbanized, theatrical, emotivist, and indeed *expressivist* view of the self and of personal life.

In the *first* place, it brings the self and the cosmos back into harmony with each other, as microcosm and macrocosm, the 'little world' and the 'great world'. Both are fountains: in both, be-ing is a continual pouring-out and passing-away.

In the *second* place, it gives us an interesting emotivist account of the philosophical quest, which has been described as 'the attempt to find reasons for what one believes instinctively'. Many people who have devoted their whole lives to the study of philosophy and theology will, I hope, agree with me that one tries to find out, and to spell out, not what one has been *told* to believe, but what (after much soul-searching) one really thinks and feels in one's own heart. Finding one's own voice is much the same in philosophy and in religious thought as it is in art. Since the emotions ultimately power everything in personal life, I will if I am honest eventually settle upon the symbols and the system of thought that best draws out my feelings and gives them reasonably coherent and unified expression. This is the vision of the world and of the human condition in which I can come to rest and feel content – for the present, at least. Then I look for arguments, and they will be definable as ways of commending my vision to you.

Notice the similarity between art and philosophy on this account. In both vocations, one is trying to find one's own voice, first learning the tradition in which one stands, and then struggling hard to develop an original personal style. In art one may seek to create a work that sits in public space and is available to others, whereas in religion one attempts to make something like art out of one's own expressive living, just now.

In the *third* place, notice that the move towards an emotive/expressivist view of personal living shifts one, both in ethics and in religion, away from all 'realist' ideas of conformity to authoritative and objective standards – 'the moral law', 'orthodox belief' – and towards a practice of living authentically, and from the heart, or wholeheartedly. From the emotivist point of view that I am trying to commend, belief-religion is dead. It cannot help us any more. Under today's cultural conditions our greatest single need is to find a way of coinciding *exactly* with our own transient, outpouring lives. We want to be able to say a Great Amen to our own lives as we live them. We want to be able to say Yes to life, or (as ordinary people correctly say) we need to be able to *live life to the full* while we have it. We need to be able to discard the 'Church' kind of religion that was merely believed, and instead take up solar living and the 'Kingdom' type of religion that is simply lived. When we fully and exactly coincide with our own living Now, there is no need for any 'beliefs' and the religious quest is over. Ordinary living is enough for us.

8

The Fountain: God's Self-Outpouring and Self-Scattering

In the old pre-Enlightenment culture it was generally assumed that the very first human beings had found themselves, in the moment of their creation, to be already well-groomed, language-using, rational adults, suddenly in a world ready made for them. In Christian art, Adam is newly shaven and Eve has a fashionable hairstyle. They are not a bit like 'cavemen'. Both are white, smooth-skinned, good-looking, very clean and well-fed. They are in a state of original righteousness and communion with God, because in those days it was assumed that the beginning of everything was a Golden Age. Since the basic ideas of philosophy, religion and ethics were believed to be timelessly true, it was assumed that the earliest and most perfect humans, being perfectly rational, would already have been in full possession of them all.

While people thought like that they could not be receptive to the idea that all human religious ideas are cultural, and have slowly developed from very primitive origins. To us, it seems obvious that our language is not timeless and sacred, having been God's possession from all eternity, but is an evolving human tool of communication, which has always been fully bound in with our own current way of life. But while people believed that God him-self actually thought, and created the world, in classical Hebrew,[18]

---

18 The Golem in Jewish legend was a clay model of a human being which an heretical Rabbi had brought to life by speaking Hebrew words over it. According to a well-known story, King James I caused an infant to be sent out to the Western Isles of Scotland, to be raised by deaf and dumb parents. A few years later a small delegation was sent to find out what had happened. They returned (so it is alleged) with the news the King wanted to hear – that the child indeed spoke a little Hebrew.

and that the Hebrew language was therefore originally *natural* to human beings, they tended to think of the words of the Bible as the words of God, and as supra-historical.

There was a minority report. Lucretius (*De Rerum Natura*, Of the Nature of Things, *c.*60–5 BC) has an excellent evolutionary account of human origins in general and human language in particular. Almost equally good is the Scotsman James Burnet, Lord Monboddo (*Of the Origin and Progress of Language*, 1774–92). By the time Darwin published *The Descent of Man* (1871), some fossil remains of early hominids such as Neanderthal man (1856) had become available, and it was quite clear that the older ideas about religion and its functions in our lives must be drastically revised.

On the newer view, then, there were not simply two first parents. There was a very long period of slow development, which we may think of as having occupied many tens of thousands, or even millions of years. During this period the earliest humans – who were of more than one species – were bipedal, with opposed thumbs and relatively large brains. They were anatomically capable of language for a long period before they had developed anything like one of our complex modern languages. A complete natural language, such as one of those that we have now, already carries within it at least a *fairly* unified world-view and a *fairly* unified selfhood (I am here referring to the skill in using indexical pronouns which gives to each of us the consciousness of being an individual self-aware person among others in a little social world, set within a larger natural world). On strictly philosophical grounds it would seem, therefore, that selfhood like ours and languages like ours probably appeared only in Middle-Palaeolithic times. Before then, there was a very long traditional and proto-linguistic period of some hundreds of thousands of years.

In short, becoming a human being, conscious, and conscious of being with others, and set in a world in which one must act, with others, to maintain one's own life and to raise the next generation – all that was very hard work indeed for the earliest humans. Far from finding themselves endowed with all the basic ideas from the first, they had a long hard struggle to work it all out. And they had no help at all.

In this long struggle, the making of human beings, religious ideas functioned as *leading* ideas. They were means by which we could get a hold of ideas about selfhood, language, the world, law, action and property which were currently right out of our own reach. So they were first ascribed to gods and spirits. For example, in Genesis God is presented as the very first subject or self, who is faced with a chaotic Other, and who knows that he must use language to divide it up into a Cosmos with various distinct regions, which must then be populated with appropriate creatures – in biblical terms, the birds of the air, the beasts of the field, and the fishes of the sea. So the idea of 'God' was a *bonne à penser*, a device to think with, that taught us how *we* could learn to build and populate our own world; and in the story God himself makes this latter point by leaving it to Adam to name the beasts. Having personally demonstrated the world-ordering power of language, God directs man to use it too. God was originally born, as he later lived and died, just for us. His function was to show us how to become ourselves.

Similarly, then, God was the first to be able to see the world not as terrifying and chaotic, but as fully formed, regular and beautiful. God imposes a régime of law upon phenomena. We will have to do the same. And God was similarly the first landlord, and the first to choose to give up nomadism and settle down in a permanent stone dwelling in a city. Above all, God was the first historical agent, who knows how to shape world-events and guide them towards the fulfilment of a great moral purpose.[19]

---

19 All this is part of the new *secular* Grand Narrative, telling of God's birth, life, and death for our redemption, that I have been attempting to spell out in recent books, including especially *Theology's Strange Return*, London: SCM Press, 2010, and *A New Great Story*, Salem, OR: Polebridge Press, 2010.

More generally, it was through religion that we taught ourselves how to structure space and time, for example by developing the Calendar, the liturgical year with its cycle of feasts and fasts, and the matching annual cycle of agricultural tasks. Ideas of a divinely given moral law, of sin and of divine judgement and punishment similarly helped to guide the development of codes of civil law, and a civil penal system with a graduated tariff of penalties. And finally, the religious hierarchization of reality prepared the way for the organization of human society, the class system and the State.

Very interestingly – if in somewhat coded form – the Hebrew Bible presents us with a detailed and complex picture that shows us how God led his people's intellectual and cultural development, gradually teaching them everything. Religion was 'our old loving nurse', and the universal educator. How else could a nervous, jumpy animal ever have got hold of the very idea of a world-picture, and the idea that moral action in a world, and in collaboration with others, is possible? Only religion could make us human.

There is more yet: in order to function as a genuinely *leading* idea, God must be a continually moving process, rather than a static timeless infinite substance. Human culture developed historically, and perhaps is still developing, by a continual progressive democratization of religious ideas. For example, the Old Testament prophets' oracles about the nations turn progressively into the New Testament's Day of Pentecost and the Gentile Church, and then into Catholicism and Ecumenicalism, and then into the League of Nations, the United Nations Organization, and finally into today's liberal multiculturalism. God continually democratizes himself and dies, as ideas that originally belonged only to God and to his ideal, eschatological future are appropriated by humans and made into part of our own everyday reality. But this continual 'death' of God by democratization, as God becomes human and is distributed through the human world, has to be balanced by a continual pushing of the God-ideal higher and higher, so that God stays firmly ahead of us and continues to lure us forward. To work, the god-idea must *both* be one full jump ahead of us, *and* attainable.

In the modern West God was pushed up into ideality by Kant, and then into the whole unfolding cosmic march of Mind by Hegel. In postmodernity there's a certain tendency to equate God with the glitter and the fertility of the endless 'play' of language and interpretation – the 'dance' of Nietzsche and Matisse. Here I am trying to suggest that religion, and human development generally, reach their highest culmination in the preaching of 'solar living' and pure love, which frees us completely from anxiety and dread about contingency and death by teaching us how to live by self-giving, and so by dying all the time. Like God, again. Love is the conquest of death by absolute generosity of spirit.

So the whole fountain is in the end God: always passing away and dying, and always renewing itself. Nothing metaphysical, nothing absolute, but only ordinary silent rushing secular contingency, lived out ethically as generous self-giving love. Like Juliet when she says: 'The more I give, the more I have', we learn that if we can learn to love life fearlessly, life will keep on bearing us up. That's It. That's all.

9

The Outpouring Human Self: The Heart

'The heart' is a very complex and no doubt much-overused metaphor. Against the background of my generally expressivist outlook, I use the terms 'heart' and 'living by the heart' to describe the complex, many-stranded, and highly sensitive outflow of libido or life-feeling by which we all of us live.

The central idea here is not new. Galen's theory of humours – sanguine, phlegmatic, choleric and melancholy – was very similar, and so too in ordinary language is talk of our 'spirits', which may be 'high', or 'good', or 'low', or 'depressed'. Freud gave a Darwinian-romantic twist to the old theme by talking of our instinctual drives (*Triebe*) and of the Id (*Es*). The Id is roughly R. L. Stevenson's Mr Hyde, or 'the beast beneath the skin'. The vocabulary in which I continue this ancient theme reflects the huge modern expansion of the use of the word 'life' – for example in such stock phrases as 'the feeling of being alive', 'the joys of life', and 'full of life'. 'The heart' is that part of us out of which 'the feeling of being alive', an emotional rush, flows forth continuously. I have called it many-stranded, and follow the 'dynamic depth-psychologists'[20] in pointing out that some of its various strands come in opposed pairs such as tenderness/violence and love/jealousy. When one of a pair is pressed too hard it may suddenly tip over into the other. Hence talk of a 'rebound', and of Hell as

---

20 This is a good term for the work of Freud and Jung, and their generation of psychological theorists. The all-important idea of the self as a less-than-harmonious system of *forces* which seek expression, and need some reconciliation, is derived by them chiefly from Schopenhauer and Nietzsche.

having 'no Fury like a woman scorn'd'. That's the sudden, shocking violence of the rebound.

In general, our life-feeling seeks to flow easily out into expression, whether direct, or symbolic, or substituted. When all our feeling-life is flowing easily and harmoniously we may be almost unaware of it. It does not trouble us, and we are aware only of contentment and absorption in the daily living of our lives: of Spinoza's 'joy, love, sanity and freedom', and of 'the affirmative emotions'. But our feeling-life can be subject to severe disturbance both for internal and for external reasons. Internally, our feelings are very liable to displacement or to trauma, as Freud taught, and they may become tangled, 'mixed' or 'conflicted'. As a result we may experience various degrees of chronic distress, and there is little agreement in detail about how best we can then restore an easy, harmonious and painless flow of our feeling-life, except that time is a great healer, and talk helps. A psychotherapist friend recently assured me that there are around 5,000 different brands in his business – a number even larger than the number of distinct Christian and Christian-related sects (which is, I think, a mere 2,000 or so).

Externally, our feelings come out into public expression in language or in other forms of symbolic behaviour; and here again our feeling-life is very acutely sensitive. It may be enhanced or dulled by what it meets. We evaluate everything, every word and every experience, sometimes sharing and sometimes not quite sharing the 'face-valuation' with which it is presented to us. There are extreme cases. For example, if it happens that I really like what I meet, my flow of feeling may be suddenly enhanced as I am 'turned on' by it. Alternatively, my response may be meek, if I am an extreme conformist who goes along passively with the valuations of everything that are presented to me by others every day. On everything, I just feel with the mass. But at the opposite extreme, I may be an extreme dissenter, someone very alienated from his contemporaries who feels differently from them about everything. It is acutely painful, because emotionally frustrating, to be entirely at odds with one's *milieu*.

There is a further complication in that the buzz of public discourse goes on continually, and nowadays with very great intensity, so that the prevailing consensus about all matters of fact, and of faith, and of moral and aesthetic value-feeling, is shifting continuously. Trendy people are sensitive to the shift, and go along with it. Critical thinkers are at all times ready to rethink their own personal convictions and feeling-valuations, and may attempt personally by arguments and interpositions to push the public consensus in one direction or another – for of course it must be stressed here that although I am an emotivist in my understanding of the self and of how we should live, I am *not* an irrationalist. It is perfectly possible to conduct a rational appraisal of the way you, or I, feel about something, and to argue that a somewhat different attitude or feeling-response might be more appropriate. Hence the possibility, and indeed the usefulness, of 'cognitive behaviour therapy' as it is called. Many of our feeling-responses are amenable to argument. They are something like 'propositional attitudes', which is why we speak of 'feeling *that*'.

We have now sketched enough background to be able to state a number of general doctrines about the self, about life, and about how we should live. We are picturing the whole of things, the Macrocosm, the Great World, as a silent, ceaselessly outpouring Fountain of formless and purely contingent be-ing, that comes forth and passes away. The Real is just pure transience. There's nothing else. And the human self is correspondingly pictured as a matching Little World or Microcosm, a complex many-stranded outpouring of biological feeling-life that similarly comes forth all the time. It gets clothed in words and their associated feeling-tones. Thus it enters the general flux of human communication – the world's consciousness of itself, the buzz – and passes away.

People who are committed either to dogmatic metaphysics or to dogmatic religious belief will think that on my account nothing is eternal and nothing is objectively real. On the contrary, everything flickers and passes away as rapidly as a movie. Everything is just a passing show, and is ultimately utterly meaningless. I ask such people to stay with me a while, for having given my revised version of ontology, or the doctrine of Creation, I now go on to revise ethics, or what in religious terms might be called the doctrines of the Fall and of Redemption.

Our greatest need as human beings is to be able to live out our transient lives *wholeheartedly* and as purely affirmatively as is consistently possible. I want to coincide exactly with my own transient life, and I want to feel my own life to be in full harmony with the outpouring, equally transient life of the Whole. When this is fully the case, I live like God in a *Nunc Stans*, a perpetual Now, at the centre of everything. So God's *Nunc Stans* is, again, the prototype for ours. That's the best there could possibly be for me, and for everyone else too. It is solar living, eternal life in the midst of pure transience. As people say, it is living life 'to its fullest'.

Just to state this doctrine is to see the need for a complete revolution in our received ideas about ethics. From our past we have inherited a conception of the ethical as an externally imposed quasi-sacred constraint upon us, which obliges us. It is our *duty*, and it is conceived of as being objective, universal and lawlike. The distinctive character of the ethical – its 'universal prescriptivity', as one writer calls it – is illustrated by the prominence in it of the 'What-if-everyone-were-to-behave-in-that-way?' type of argument. The ethical (on this interpretation of it) is highly rational: it's a matter of what we can think of as being anyone's and everyone's plain duty in such and such a situation. Personal feeling is irrelevant, as is pointed out by drawing a sharp contrast between duty and inclination, between what I *know* I *ought* to do and what I *feel* I'd *like* to do.

The most famous ethic of this type – 'duty for duty's sake' – is that proposed by Kant.[21] On his view, there is nothing ethically

---

21 Best set out in his *Groundwork of the Metaphysic of Morals*, 1789. The standard commentaries, both much too respectful, are by H. J. Paton and Sir David Ross.

admirable at all in a mother's feeding her baby because she loves it. She is morally praiseworthy only if she would have fed the baby anyway, whether she loved it or not, but simply because she knows it's her *duty* to feed it.

And here one rebels, as many of Kant's early readers of the Romantic generation rebelled. His ethic seems all-too masculinist, disciplinarian, and Teutonic. It is far too self-controlled and authoritarian, and as we all know such a psychology can easily go horribly wrong. Who today wants to be like that; and indeed who today could want a normal *woman* to be like that? One starts to suspect that the whole ethical tradition, going back to Plato (and also to the great lawgivers of religion) has always been too hostile to the emotions. The reason/emotion contrast is just as deeply embedded in our culture, and just as objectionable now, as all the other binary oppositions, between material and spiritual, between appearance and reality, and so forth.

Ethics is in a mess. It needs a revolution. A good and straightforward starting-point can be found by simply looking up and re-reading the splendidly direct and forceful speeches of Jane Eyre, in the romantic novel of that name by Charlotte Brontë (1847), to Rochester and to St John Rivers.

Everyone knows the outbursts to Rochester, so let us here consider the unfortunate Rivers.[22] He is a Cambridge man, a clergyman of the noblest character, who is going to India as a missionary. He needs a helpmeet, a sort of curate, through whose work as a primary-school teacher he can get access to Hindu women. The ideal helpmeet will need to be a wife who shares his high ideals. So it is to him clearly God's will that he should ask Jane to marry him, and that she should assent to his proposal.

The debate this opens between them is lengthy and complicated. Jane respects and even shares St John Rivers' idealism,

---

22 Read the second half of Chapter XXXIV for the splendid demolition of Rivers by Jane.

and even declares herself very willing to serve as his colleague. But marry him she will not, and when he presses his argument she becomes on occasion sarcastic and scornful to a degree that he never expected to encounter in a woman. 'I scorn your ideal of love,' she says, 'I scorn the counterfeit sentiment you offer: yes, St John, and I scorn you when you offer it.' In an earlier meditation on Rivers' offer Jane says to herself:

> He prizes me as a soldier would a good weapon, and that is all … Can I bear the consciousness that every endearment he bestows is a sacrifice made on principle? No: such a martyrdom would be monstrous. I will never undergo it …

Jane Eyre the novel may be early Victorian melodrama with a preposterous plot, but the moral point Jane herself makes is perfectly sound. A man who proposes marriage to a woman needs to persuade her that his love for her is overriding and wholehearted. Otherwise, it is morally odious. In our culture it has long, and rightly, been accepted that a person of either sex may quite properly be ready to change even his or her *religion* for the sake of a marriage. Just human sexual object-choice, seeking marriage, may be more important than God! It matters *that much*, and to suggest to a woman that you are proposing to her for instrumental reasons is to offer her a profound insult. No: the rules of the game are clear: the man must be utterly serious, and then for her part the woman can be relied upon to do him the honour of taking him seriously, however implausible a suitor he may appear to be. And that's how it works. Rivers is, tragically, totally incapable of understanding the point because he is an orthodox Augustinian, who believes in the *ordo amoris*, the rule that you should love each thing according to its rank in the cosmic scale of being. God most of all, and then other things for God's sake, and in due order. So he believes that he and Jane, living together as man and wife, and working together on the mission field, can fit their mutual love as man and wife, and as colleagues, into the larger and greater context of their doing the Will of God.[23] And Jane won't buy that, and Jane is right. Rivers gets the earful he deserves.

To avoid a possible misunderstanding at this point I need to acknowledge that in the old Plato-to-Kant tradition – a tradition in which Kierkegaard, anachronistically, still stood – the word 'heart' was often used in the sense of your real, deep down, *rational intention*, your will. Hence talk of 'purity of heart', meaning purity or singleness of mind, or intention, or will. The reference is to the rational consistency of a person who really is, all the way down, what he or she purports to be. In the modern idiom: 'What you see is what you get'. But as I said at the outset I am not using the word 'heart' to mean *voluntas*, the will: I am using it to mean the source, and the flowing-out from that source, of our *libido*, or life-feeling, or emotions. (This, because there are not two things, the source and the outflow, for they are one and the same. There is only the flowing-out.) We are happiest and most at one with ourselves and with 'it all' when the outflow of our feeling into symbolic action and communication with others is easiest and most direct and forceful. We are happiest when we are most contentedly absorbed in life – which, as Freud sagely observes, consists largely of 'love and work'. In personal ethics we should aim to live as generously and as consistently affirmatively as we can, cultivating magnanimity and the affirmative emotions. Only a very exceptional person could hope to live without any negative emotion, or *ressentiment*, but we should certainly try never to allow such emotions to stick to us and to fester, for they poison the soul.

When did we change over from using 'the heart' to mean 'what deep down we really will, or intend' to the more modern emotivist meaning of 'the heart' as the source of an outpouring of libido, or life-feeling? The great original pioneer is Spinoza. Every

---

23 In Latin Christian moral theology, which has always been written by celibate males who have no idea of what a serious matter sexual love can and should be, the sin of inordinate love of one's wife is 'uxoriousness'.

use of the word 'heart' by the younger Wordsworth deserves study, as does Darwin's wonderfully observant work on *The Expression of the Emotions in Men and Animals* (1872). Then came the moderns, some or most of them rather out of fashion just now: Nietzsche, Freud, D. H. Lawrence and so on. A good example of the full arrival of the modern revaluation of the emotions is the Scottish Hegelian-Quaker philosopher John Macmurray, who in his *Reason and Emotion* (1935) redefines chastity as 'emotional sincerity'.

From this starting-point we can next attempt a slightly more detailed account of personal or 'lifestyle' ethics, or 'spirituality' (as I prefer *not* to call it). As for social ethics, or the ethics of justice, I see it as primarily a matter to be sorted out within the general public conversation about politics and the resolution of disputes. The principles involved are not specially profound: they are known to all parents who have raised a family of bickering, squabbling children, and who know the arguments and the tricks one must use to persuade them all that each of them is getting a fair deal and should not waste time worrying that someone else may be getting a slightly larger slice of cake than they are. I don't want to make a great fuss about justice: it's a matter merely of mutual *adjustment*. As such, it is no doubt a matter about which we'll go on bickering for ever, though not because it is a matter of any great profundity, but merely because children love to squabble.

10

The Outpouring Human Self: The Criterion of Morality

For most of human history religion has been telling human beings that in order to rise to their full potential they must distance themselves as much as possible from all other animals and from everything animal in their own makeup. You are human, we were told, that is, you are a rational being and a moral agent. You have an immortal rational soul, and your will is free. Therein lies your whole dignity. And against this background religious and philosophical thought paid little or no attention to the body, the senses, the passions, and sex and reproduction. The tendency to a form of 'angelism'[24] was so strong that in many traditions it came to be believed that the best life of all for a human being to live was a life that had almost completely dropped out of nature, and out of ordinary human historical life in time. Monks and nuns spent their days enclosed within stone walls, in a kind of antechamber to eternity where they devoted themselves to the contemplative life.

Nowadays most people think of religious belief as irrational – a misconception, because several traditions, and especially Latin and Greek Christianity, in fact suffered from a crazily excessive rationalism which always was and still is very damaging to ordinary human beings. A fightback by the poets on behalf of women, human love, and secular family life began in the Western towns during the high Middle Ages, but in ethical theory even a

---

24 The term 'angelism' is sometimes used to ridicule an ethic or recommended way of life that pretends that a human being can live like an angel, entirely disregarding and denying his or her own animal nature.

figure as important as Kant himself was still wildly rationalistic in the late eighteenth century.

Against this background, the general drift of my present argument is clear. Where Kant finds his criterion of morality in *rational* consistency and integrity of the will, I am proposing to find mine in *emotional* authenticity, directness and integrity. My action is truly mine and truly moral in insofar as it is inspired by my own sincere and generous feeling. I really *mean* it. But I must hasten to repeat that I see social ethics, the ethics of justice, as a matter in which, through legal debate and the ongoing public political conversation, we seek to establish and to keep in repair an acceptable public consensus. So much for social ethics. There's nothing very special or difficult about it: it's a matter of bargaining. But personal ethics, or the ethics of love, or 'spirituality', is more challenging. From my animal background I have inherited very acute senses, passions that are all too quickly aroused, inflamed, and (often) displaced, and a nervous highly strung nature which is made still more keyed up and anxiety-prone by my human consciousness (that is, all those words racing through my head). I really need to be able to get myself together as a human animal, and therefore I need to find ways of avoiding the traditional bipolar splitting of the self between reason and emotion, sense and spirit, justice and love, short-term and long-term, duty and inclination, and so on.

In search of a more unified and expressive selfhood, I reflect that (as is often said) reason by itself moves nothing. It may be the steering-wheel but it is not itself the engine. So a fully modern and post-Darwinian ethic will be emotivist. If I can get my feelings straightened out and flowing harmoniously, if I can find a genuinely affirmative relation to life (a 'positive attitude', people may say), then I can act morally. My feelings will flow easily out into symbolic expression in words and deeds, and will be authentically and identifiably my own, insofar as I can by my words and deeds directly affirm love for life in general, and for my fellow-being in particular, in the various roles I play in the daily living of my life. That's the model for right moral action in personal ethics: it is that one should learn to live 'by the heart', or by love. It is not the traditional *contemplative* life; it is the *communicative* life.

It is evident at once that an emotive-expressivist approach to personal ethics will reject outright every kind of ethical heteronomy. No external code of religious law, whether thought of as built into the way Nature goes, or as revealed in the Bible, or as deducible from the bare concept of a rational agent (Aquinas, Calvin, and Kant respectively), none of these can teach me to live by the heart the life of love. I have to learn that for myself, and it will usually involve the use of self-criticism, psychotherapy, prayer, or meditation – whatever I may need in order to get myself sorted out so that my tangled feelings can flow more easily, and I can learn to enjoy life and to exchange love easily.

Ordinary language, as it has developed especially since about the time of D. H. Lawrence, is already full of interesting emotivist/expressivist idioms, often entertainingly liquid, as when we speak of *bottled-up feelings*, of *betraying our true feelings*, of a *giveaway* and of *self-revelation*, or of a *letting slip* that *says it all*. In a confessional mood, one may *pour out one's heart, let it all hang out*, and *make a clean breast of it* or *get it off one's chest*. After the catharsis of releasing our feelings, we may be more able to speak of *a change of heart*, and to make use of personal idioms like *with all my heart*, and *put your heart into it* (as opposed to the very interesting and significant *I haven't the heart to …*).

Now a further gain from the switch to an emotivist understanding of ethics: it has us thinking in terms of process and time and role-play from the outset. In the older philosophical tradition one operated with a marked preference for, and orientation towards, the eternal world, and still for Kant philosophy kept its gaze fixed upon the old world of *a priori* truth, things that are true always, and *before* this world of time and change. So Kant, weirdly, has basically timeless ideas of the moral agent, reason, freedom, principles and moral action. But nobody can think like that now, surely, and I have been stressing throughout that on my account

I, my own outpouring life, and the entire going-on of things in the human social world are one continuous streaming temporal process. Nothing's quite pure, or stable and self-identical; everything's mixed, streaming, sparkling, mutable, flowing. Gradually, as I get into the habit of thinking in the new fully temporalized way, I find I am quite getting to like it all just as it is. I no longer *want* to be an immortal soul purifying itself for eternity. I feel increasingly happy to be just a time-bound mortal. So, if it is true that the fundamental religious problem of modern people is their secret anxiety about time and their utter horror of approaching death, then it is precisely for such people that I am writing. Even if these ideas can help only one such person, I'm glad. People of my generation remember the playwright Denis Potter saying at the end of his life how overwhelmingly beautiful the everyday world of sunlight, vegetation and birdsong had become now that he was just about to leave it. In his place I would have added that since I shall never know that I am dead, there is for me only this, Now; and in this (for *me*, eternal) Now I enjoy a love and a beauty far beyond the ken of an immortal angel. I'm the one who is a whole world better off, because the eternal Now I enjoy now is present and is better than his allegedly bigger Eternal Now in Heaven.

Similarly, a thoroughgoing emotivist ethic of love gives me an exultant feeling of freedom and release that is far beyond anything attainable by a dully righteous law-abiding Kantian. When I was young, serious-minded moral philosophers strove to impress upon me the idea that emotivism was a rather disgraceful doctrine, sceptical (and probably worse; that is, *cynical*) and typically propagated by slightly *louche* characters like Freddy Ayer. I don't think that now.

11

That's It: Solar Dying

Across much of the Old World, in both Europe and Asia, it has always been a cliché both of philosophy and of religious thought that everything is contingent: everything just happens to be what it is, and nothing has to turn out as it does. It all just chances to be so, and in addition everything is transient. Everything slowly becomes more and more attenuated and widely scattered, getting thinner and colder.

During the past forty years, the dominance of the Big-Bang cosmology has greatly reinforced this ancient idea of universal contingency and transience. The entire cosmos is now seen as just a single colossal event – an explosion and a prolonged scattering, cooling and decay. And if that is how things are, then there is no way of incorporating our current cosmology into any kind of optimistic Grand Narrative or cosmic story of Fall and Redemption, or conflict and resolution. Any large-scale Happy Ending for us all appears to be ruled out.

It may of course be pointed out that the cosmic Bang is so vast, and the whole process of explosion and scattering so complex, that it is possible for local irregularities to 'feed' upon the scattering energies around them for a while, rather as little eddies and whirlpools may develop in small pools along the course of a white-water cascading river. You and I and our whole planet are examples of such interesting by-products or side-effects of the slowly unwinding Bang.

However, there's a further complication. During the first half of the nineteenth century a big collaborative effort of geologists established the succession of the rock strata in the earth's crust, and also the succession of different fossilized plant and animal species within the strata. As a fine passage in Tennyson's *In Memoriam A. H. H.* (1850) shows, this was a severe shock to people who had hitherto believed that God had created a fixed and complete set of animal and plant species, headed by the human species, which would together populate the Earth from Creation to Doomsday. It now appeared that every species, including Man, was destined to be around for only a limited period before it became extinct. This put paid to the traditional notion that the earth and every species of plant and animal upon it had been specially created to function as a more-or-less unchanging stage-set for human history. Instead it now appears that we are temporary and accidental side-effects of a mighty cosmic process that isn't going anywhere and cares nothing for us.

Are God and Nature then at strife,
    That Nature lends such evil dreams?
    So careful of the type, she seems,
So careless of the single life ...

'So careful of the type?' but no.
    From scarped cliff and quarried stone
    She cries, 'A thousand types are gone:
I care for nothing, all shall go.

Thou makest thine appeal to me:
    I bring to life, I bring to death:
    The spirit does but mean the breath:
I know no more.' And he, shall he,

Man, her last work, who seem'd so fair,
    Such splendid purpose in his eyes,
    Who rolled the psalm to wintry skies,
Who built him fanes of fruitless prayer,

Who trusted God was love indeed

And love Creations final law –
Tho' Nature, red in tooth and claw
With ravine, shrieked against his creed –

Who loved, who suffer'd countless ills,
Who battled for the True, the Just,
Be blown about the desert dust,
Or seal'd within the iron hills?

(from sections lv, lvi)

In time, Man will become extinct, and as Ruskin, Tennyson and others testify, it was the geologist's hammer tapping at the rocks and building up the fossil record that, as much as anything else, brought about the mid-century and middle-class crisis of faith. Even to this day conservative Evangelical Protestants still insist that the modern purpose-free and value-neutral scientific world-picture makes human life utterly insignificant and 'meaningless'. There are some scientists who are spiritually tough, and speak with a kind of gloomy relish about the future extinction of the human species – already certain in the very long run, and now perhaps less than two or three centuries away. But to the Evangelicals, and (they think) to the great majority of ordinary people, this modern scientific world picture is utterly terrifying, so bad that it is, they think, quite clearly 'too bad to be true'. Hence the aggressiveness of the fundamentalist revolt. They *must* fight very hard to reinstate the old Protestant 'assurance' about God and his Plan of Salvation for us, because the alternative is for them too bad to be borne.

A third point needs to be added to complete the present argument. As originally proposed, Darwin's theory had a number of weaknesses – especially those that resulted from his lack of genetic theory. But after it had been found that the main raw material of evolution is genetic mutations, which are typically recessive, and not random variations as Darwin himself had taught, the problem arose of how a favourable mutation could succeed in spreading through a whole population and becoming dominant. This tricky question was successfully answered by R. A. Fisher, and by the late 1930s, a neo-Darwinian synthesis was established and has not been seriously challenged since. Indeed, the huge development of biochemistry has very strongly confirmed it. There is then no good reason to doubt the basic machinery of Darwinism, except for one point. His use of the metaphor of 'selection' seems to suggest a choice by a stockbreeder with a goal in view; and that is unfortunate, because in fact Darwin remained, and biology generally remains, mechanistic. There is no Selector. The process is not in any way 'teleological' or goal-oriented. Where large numbers of organisms of the same species are competing to survive, those that do survive will tend to be those best fitted to do so – and that's all.

I make this latter point because too many religious apologists still claim that Darwinism is compatible with belief in God. But if 'belief in God' entails belief that a moral providence watches over all events in Nature and guides them towards a predestined and morally grand conclusion, then it has to be said, for the sake of truth, that, No: Darwinism is certainly *not* compatible with a fully traditional belief in a Divine Providence that watches over every single individual sparrow. The Process does not care about the individual – whereas we do, and should.

It seems then to be almost certain that we can no longer look to the earthly and cosmic future for a better world, and we can no longer claim to have good reasons to believe that there is a better heavenly world that awaits us 'after' death. (I put the word 'after' in scare quotes to remind the reader that there is no common time-scale (nor indeed any 'landmark' or 'timemark') linking this world and the supposed post-mortem world. The two worlds are discontinuous, so that we have no way of talking meaningfully about *continuing* subjective life in another world *after* death.) It seems to follow therefore that the self and the cosmos remain in step, as they do in most systems of thought, so that nowadays both just peter out. Neither has any great long-tem 'expectations' (to use a Victorian term).

Let's try to put it still more plainly: none of us has any good reason to hope that the general conditions of human existence, or our religious state, or just my own state of life, will ever be notably better than they are now. There is no Better World to come on earth, and no Better World awaiting us after death. The best I can hope for is a slow and not-too-painful decline for a few years yet.

Grasping this with perfect clarity, Nietzsche concluded correctly that we need to find a way of saying a full and wholehearted Yes to life in the here and now. We'll never have a better chance of finding eternal happiness than we have today. Whereas historical faith looked ahead to find its final goal, post-historical faith concludes that we have no future, and seeks to concentrate attention upon the present.

A few people reached similar conclusions in antiquity, including especially the Epicurean Atomists who culminated in Lucretius. The serenity (*ataraxia*) with which Epicurus himself had viewed life and faced death must have been the model for the good-humour with which David Hume received visitors to his own deathbed in 1776.[25]

You may be unimpressed. After all, edifying stories about how philosophers have faced death 'philosophically' have been common ever since Socrates. Other people who have not devoted their lives to philosophy may find it more difficult to view their own fast-approaching extinction quite so calmly. They may find it more helpful to hear about those religious traditions, Protestant Christian and Mahayana Buddhist, which offer a way to sudden salvation in the present moment. In Christianity the original sixteenth-century Lutheran formula, 'Justification by faith alone' made the laborious Catholic way to salvation by a very long path of self-purification and ascetical living suddenly unnecessary. Luther therefore could renounce his religious vows and marry his

---

25 See Boswell's account, reprinted in Norman Kemp South's classic edition of Hume's *Dialogues Concerning Natural Religion*, London: Nelson, 1947; US reprint, Indianapolis: Bobbs-Merrill, 1962.

Katharina von Bora, a former nun, in 1525. He fathered six children, and never knew that a Japanese Buddhist monk named Shinran had done all the same things just 300 years earlier. Shinran (1173–1262) lived at a time when it was widely thought that a corrupt world was hastening to its end. One must seize salvation fast, and could do so by an act of simple faith in Amitabha (or Amida) Buddha. That done, it was no longer necessary to be a monk, and Shinran married and lived a secular life in the world.

Thus within the great faith-traditions themselves there has long been a possibility of discarding asceticism and the entire apparatus of mediated, institutional, long-termist religion. Instead, one can find eternal happiness right now, in the present moment, by simply setting aside one's own future (or lack thereof), and saying a wholehearted yes to this transient life of ours, now.

Ideas of this kind not only have a long history in poetry, but also figure prominently now in ordinary language. People who have made a good recovery from life-threatening illness, or who have reached retirement age, typically speak of *treating life as a gift, taking each day as it comes*, and of *living for the moment*. People who say this sort of thing have come to see that it is a mistake to spend one's entire life in putting up with oppression and hardship for the sake of a glorious recompense hereafter. Toiling away, trusting a promise, living in hope, is not really living at all. We will be frittering away the only life we'll ever have in yearning for an imaginary better world. And then, suddenly, bright sunshine on a summer morning says: All this, now! – and the cobwebs are blown away, and we are abruptly filled with happiness. It's the theme of a thousand poems, and every one of them is quite correct.

Which reminds me that the Fountain is non-historical. It streams and sparkles in the sunshine, now. It is a symbol of life's endlessly self-renewing energy and sweetness. Just to see and to recognize *that* is all that we can have as death closes in. And I guess now that that is the point of the end of Tolstoy's celebrated story, *The Death of Ivan Ilyich* (1884). Ilyich is a civil servant, an ordinary man struck down with a mortal illness and fighting desperately against it. He rages on and on. Gradually his resistance breaks down, and he is able to accept death only by affirming life with his last breath. All of life's heartbreaking beauty lies *precisely* in its transience. It takes a long time and a hard struggle to say that – to say that life and death are a package deal. Say an all-out yes to the one, and you've accepted the other, too. *You've made it.*

12

Reserved Business

Wittgenstein once remarked to his friend Con Drury that 'The religion of the future will have to be very ascetical – and by that I don't mean only in matters of food and drink.' I think it is clear that Wittgenstein was saying that in our post-metaphysical times, when the scope of philosophy cannot be wider than the scope of ordinary language, religion needs to be *intellectually* austere and reticent. Religious teaching cannot and must not pretend to give us any extra supernatural information about how things are for us, and what may be in store for us. All it can pretend to do is to rearrange our thoughts, cure us of certain perplexities and discomforts, and reconcile us to the basic facts of life that all of us already know.

So far, in this present 'secular theology', I have tried to stick to that rule. I do not have anything fresh to report (for example, about the existence of a supernatural world, about God, and about life after death). I do not have any real *news*. Instead, I have stuck rigidly to the simplest facts of life. For example, I have said that it is clearly the case that it is possible nowadays for life to be pretty good for most people in a tolerably well-governed country. Most people can enjoy a full span of life. Much can be done to reduce traditional threats to our happiness. Wonderful cultural riches and natural beauties are available to us all every day. But we all of us remain vulnerable to various sorts of suffering and distress, either arising endogenously within ourselves or inflicted upon us by external factors, and we all remain as vulnerable as ever to sickness, ageing, decline and death. Whether we have been lucky or unlucky in life, we all know that in due course everything will come to an end for each one of us. Contingency, transience and death are as much a problem for modern people as they were for the young Siddhartha Gautama when he was first struck by them twenty-five centuries ago.

At this point my 'theology' did not seek to *escape* from transience and death; instead we positively *dwelt* upon them. In our time the development of thought and of our new technologies has surrounded us with images of everything as pouring out into expression and passing away – broadcasted, scattered, disseminated. We have looked at examples: the silent outpouring of all be-ing, our Big-Bang cosmology, the energetic perpetual striving and self-renewal of all life, the human self as intensely and continuously expressive and communicative, and the good life as an 'outgoing' life of emotional expression, the life of love. We have used the Fountain as a traditional unifying and reconciling symbol: it is all pure streaming formless contingency, but at the same time it is also restful, life-giving, and a blissful object of contemplation. So we may be able to see religion, not as an attempt to gain release from time and transience, but as a way of merging ourselves into and actively affirming the universal transience that we contemplate, and in that way finding perfect happiness *now*.

Such has been our message. No extra facts: just a different way of relating ourselves to all the things about life that we all of us already know.

However, there have been a number of points in the argument at which I have felt strongly tempted to push on further, and risk breaking my own self-denying ordinance.

*   *   *

The first of them was the question of the Torus which, as I remarked above, has haunted me all my life and especially since 1994.[26] Let us briefly explain it once again.

---

26 *After All*, London: SCM Press, 1994, pp. 59f.

Draw a circle on a piece of paper, and then a second circle of the same diameter beside it, and just touching it. Label the point of contact AO. Draw a vertical line through AO. Now rotate the figure around that axis, and we have the Torus, a fat doughnut whose central hole is reduced to a bare point. That point (AO) is the initial singularity from which the Big Bang begins, arcing up and over the surface of the Torus like a fountain as the Cosmos expands. After going through 180°, the expansion-phase ends, and in the lower half of the diagram the whole Cosmos returns, back into its own origin, which is both Alpha and Omega, Big Bang and Black Hole. The entire cycle happens only once, and since the implosion-phase recovers all the energy expanded in the ex-plosion-phase, everything balances out, and the whole Torus is simultaneously made of nothing but pure streaming contingency, *and* at the same time is an eternal, blissful, self-existent whole. Since there is no external time scale, the Torus is objectively eternal, and the Eternal Return happens only once.

Such in brief summary is the 'Energetic Spinozism' that I played with in the 1990s, picturing the world as an eternal Fountain that perpetually recycles its own waters. It is not an original idea: on the contrary, it has various sources both in mythology and in modern physical theory.

In mythology, the snake was thought able perpetually to renew its own youth by shedding its skin, and a serpent devouring its own tail became a popular symbol of eternity, the Uroboros (from *drakon ouroboros*, in Greek). In physics there is, or has been, an hypothetical particle called a tachyon which travels faster than light, and therefore goes back in time to fuel the Big Bang.[27] In addition, a number of contemporary theorists are attracted by the suggestion that the present expansion-phase of cosmic history will be succeeded by a contraction-phase, leading eventually to a Big

---

27 Gregory Benford, *Timescape*, London: Gollancz, 1980. Only science fiction, of course, but it does memorably prompt one to see how a purely contingent Universe might be seen as self-existent.

Crunch. If the Going-out and the Return mirror each other closely enough, then we may be able to imagine a self-existent timeless Whole – which reminds one of classical religious visions of God and of Eternity as a great ring of light: Dante's mystic Rose, and Henry Vaughan's great 'Ring of pure and endless light'.[28]

There is, however, a difficulty. By definition, nobody can ever step out of the Whole and see it *sub specie aeternitatis* as the Whole, because it *is* the Whole, and the Whole has no outside. In which case my grandiose vision of the Whole can never be verified by *any* observer, and should be shunned as a temptation – which is why the Torus is *not* part of the main argument of the present essay. It is merely 'floated' here, like the myths in Plato. It is a story in which we seem to see some religious and philosophical gain, but we will never be in a position to check its truth. My astrophysicist friend sniffs at all such speculations. 'Not science', he says, and I guess that from my point of view I agree. In the end we don't have and never will have anything better than the sunshine I see out of my window now. All this is all there is, and we should not allow ourselves to get into the habit of indulging in long-term and large-scale fantasies.

*   *   *

The second point at which I have felt acutely tempted to push the argument further, and thereby to risk breaking my own self-denying ordinance, has to do with ethics. In *Solar Ethics* I made it clear that my own emotivist/expressivist ethics was intended to be an interpretation of Christian Ethics, but, although I quoted him, I avoided mentioning 'the man' by name.[29] More recently, in *Jesus and Philosophy* (2010) I have attempted to demonstrate, within the best available traditions of Jesus' teaching, the beginnings of

---

28 I refer to Vaughan's poem 'The World', and to the vision of God in Dante's *Paradiso*, Canto XXXIII.

29 *Solar Ethics*, London: SCM Press, 1995, p. 9.

our own post-Nietzschean radical-humanist ethics.[30] In our own day we have recently become accustomed to speaking of *human* rights rather than natural rights, and of *human* values rather than absolute values. We realize now that we are ourselves the only inventors of our own ethics. But my attempt to show the beginnings of this doctrine in Jesus himself, so long ago, was novel.

The crucial step in the argument is the one that breaks with every form of moral realism or heteronomy. I see Jesus as radicalizing the teaching of the Israelite prophets in his view that moral realism – that is, ethical heteronomy, the regulation of the moral life by an externally imposed code of religious Law – has failed to produce a good society, and will always fail. In the good society to come into being at the end of days, morality will perforce become thoroughly autonomous, and 'internalized'. Many Christian teachers make at this point the catastrophic error of supposing that Jesus is talking about the replacement of an external tyranny by an *internal* tyranny of scrupulosity. Not at all! Certainly not! Never! Jesus never uses the word conscience: he wants the moral life to become purely affirmative, spontaneous, and wholehearted. You are not a truly moral person at all unless your ethics, your way of life, is an authentic expression of your own outgoing feelings. There is no moral authority or moral order out there. *We* invent ethics. You must *not* accept any ready-made moral code, and you should forget about popular ideas of justice and your rights. You need to live generously, according to love, and in a way that is 'solar' – that is, purely affirmative and outgoing, like a lamp, or like the Sun.

Now Jesus lived in strange times. He had a very intense moral passion, with a sharp focus upon the relationship between one human being and the next, and he lived at a time when eschatological expectation was very strong. This present age was coming to an end, and we could not look to it for moral support. The better world could not be long delayed. So, in order to expedite its

---

30 *Jesus and Philosophy*, London: SCM Press, 2010.

coming, he preached that it was even now beginning, and we must choose to begin living the new kind of solar or extra-generous life right away. And it's *not* 'love your neighbour' – that's the slogan of the old order.[31] It's 'love your enemy' – and that slogan is typical of the new ethic.

In several recent books I have been trying to retell a sort-of *Christian* Grand Narrative theology. In these writings I have said that the preaching of Jesus in Galilee was the highest point in the history of religions so far.[32]

Continuing my story, the fall of the Jesus-tradition into ecclesiastical Christianity happened in the late 40s. It was associated with the leadership struggle among Jesus' surviving male followers, and in particular between Peter, James, and (a little later) the energetic and very able newcomer Paul. In the little community there was a tradition that Mary of Magdala had reported hallucinations of Jesus soon after his death. Such events are purely natural occurrences, and many widowed people report them to this day. But Peter was prompted to develop the claim that the dead Jesus had been exalted to Heaven as Messiah-designate, and would before long return to establish his kingdom upon earth. This was soon developed into the claims that Jesus had been raised from the dead and actually seen by Mary, by Peter himself, and then by others – including eventually such lowly beings as James the Lord's brother, and even Paul.[33] Now Jesus was enthroned at God's right hand as God's CEO, and an ecclesiastical epoch could be envisaged, during which the apostles, led by Peter, would rule the Church on the Lord's behalf and during the period of his absence. The actual living of the kingdom-life today was postponed further and further into the future, and Jesus' own distinctive message was forgotten. (If it had been better remembered, the tradition of it could surely not have been so badly

---

31 Leviticus 19.18.
32 See *A New Great Story*, Salem, OR: Polebridge Press, 2010.
33 For example, the account in 1 Corinthians 15.3–8.

corrupted and confused by poor-quality supplementary material as in fact it was.)

The new religion of the 50s, well-documented in the earlier Pauline Epistles, was Emergent Ur-Catholicism – the religion that slowly came to be thought of as 'Christianity'. It was a strangely eclectic compilation, combining elements of platonic philosophy, Jewish theology of history, Bronze-Age religion, and Roman methods of government. It pretty well reburied Jesus, who has only recently begun to emerge from his long ecclesiastical eclipse.

And now you see why I could not include him explicitly and by name in the central argument of this present essay – nor even in *Solar Ethics* (1995) – because if I did so I would be in danger of encouraging a repetition of the same old mistake. Do you remember Baudrillard's essays, *Forget Foucault* and *Forget Baudrillard*??[34] In the same way, if we are to preserve Jesus' teaching faithfully and transmit to the future some idea of what it was all about, then we have to forget Jesus the individual. Any cult of personality, any iconization of him, would again destroy Jesus' message. So, once again, *Forget Jesus*!

*   *   *

The third and last of these points in my main argument about which I have been tempted to become a little too explicit has to do with language and its Other, Non-language, or be-ing, or simply 'the possible'. Or, indeed, Be-ing, crossed out. If a thing's body is the organ through which it manifests itself, then language needs a body; and what can the body of language be? At this point my own thinking has never been able to escape from the old matter/form distinction, which as Derrida says 'opens philosophy', and perhaps we can indeed never wholly escape it. The linguistic sign is a Form, but what matter does it shape into a concrete word? Sometimes I

---

34 *Oublier Foucault*, Paris: Galilée, 1977, New York: Semiotext(e), 1987; *Forget Baudrillard?*, London and New York: Routledge, 1993.

have imagined e-mergent be-ing as a gentle gale, an efflux of possibilities, so that I think of language as closing down upon one set of possibilities and so fixing the world.[35] But that sounds as if language's Other is a purely logical entity, the possible, and nothing tangible or empirical at all. At other times I have thought of language's pre-existent, unFormed Other as Chaos, imagining it as the foaming speckled darkness that is before our closed eyes at night, or as the white noise emitted by an old-fashioned AM radio set when it is off tune. I rather like this analogy because I have noticed that although the speckled foam and the white noise are undoubtedly *extended*, the one in two-dimensional space and the other in time, their time and space are very ill-formed and distorted. I'm reminded of Kant, and start ruminating – until I am brought up short by remembering that any and every attempt to describe language's Other, or to describe the pre-linguistic chaos, is hopelessly paradoxical.

So I have remained a little stuck at this point. I am tempted by pure linguistic idealism, because the bigger cyberspace gets to be, and the more it comes to dominate all intellectual life, the closer we are sure to come to a revival of Hegel's Absolute Idealism. Perhaps that *is* the direction in which everything's going; but this present essay is intended to be a very general *religious* book, in which case I should not block the reader's way by insisting that you must pass through a narrow and objectionable-looking philosophical gate before you can get into the religious garden. So I have decided that I must leave this present matter at that.

*   *   *

Such then are the three questions which in this present essay I have left undetermined. The Buddha is said to have maintained that you don't need to have come to a definite view about all the ultimate questions before you can begin to walk along the path to

---

35 See Hilary Lawson, *Closure: A Story of Everything*, London: Routledge, 2001.

blessedness. He mentions questions about God, about Creation, and about the human soul's nature and destiny. I have reserved and left undetermined three topics. They are:

1 The TORUS. If we can find eternal happiness briefly within the flux of our own contingent human living, might it be possible on the large scale to see the Whole of which our own language is part as One, blessed and eternal? Can we go cosmic, and perhaps attempt a Spinozistic reinstatement of God?

2 The TEACHER. If the spirituality and life-path or ethic that I describe is in fact attributable to Jesus, why shouldn't we say so, and rebuild Christianity around him and his long-term legacy?

3 NON-LANGUAGE. Are we now moving into an epoch in which cyberspace, the 'virtual' world of communication, gets bigger and bigger, and the 'real' world steadily shrinks and finally disappears? Is it time to commit to neo-Hegelianism, or to pure linguistic idealism?

I have warned against these three questions, which means that I have after all *mentioned* them, and thereby have put temptation in your path. But the heart of the matter is solar living. Learn *that*, and everything else can be left to look after itself.

13

The Fountain of Eternal Life

Nietzsche has said that every notable philosophical system is a compressed spiritual autobiography. This, its maker is telling us, is the vision of the world in which after many years of toil I have at last felt able to come to rest. Perhaps he's saying: 'This is what suits me. Maybe, if I have spelt it all out persuasively enough, you may feel that it suits you too.'

Every philosopher – or nearly every one – is a heretic. He is a restless, questioning, critical person whose need to satisfy *himself* turns out to be stronger than his desire to continue a respected, conforming member of his own people. They, for their part, must regard him as a heretic, or even as an apostate; but one might just as well argue that the philosopher who cannot help but pursue his own quest for personal intellectual satisfaction at any cost is the most religious person of all.

To make the same point in theological terms, I knew from quite early on that I was not an ecclesiastical theologian, content to be constrained by tradition and by communal loyalty. I was always a philosophical theologian, or worse, a 'creative' theologian, an awkward animal. I cannot be discreet, I have to look for trouble, I have to be explicit, I must expose myself in public, and I had to struggle on until I felt I had found my own voice at last. Thus I ended up where I am now, telling the story that best expressed, betrays and relieves my own gut-feeling about our common human condition and how we can make the best of it.

It's taken a long time, and I have come a long way – or so it has seemed to me. I suspect that someone else, looking at my work, may conclude that I was always going to end up where I am now. I was made deacon by William Greer, Bishop of Manchester, in his

Cathedral on Trinity Sunday 1959, and ordained priest just a year later. At that time I was a typical Anglican, in the sense of being a high orthodox Christian Platonist with the usual leanings towards mild agnosticism. During the intervening half-century I have moved about as far from my starting-point as Spinoza had moved by the time when he was expelled from the Amsterdam Synagogue in 1656 at the age of 24. I haven't exactly made things easy for myself.

Why have I gone so slowly, and made such heavy weather of my journey? Spinoza is a thoroughgoing rationalist who talks much of eternity, necessity, substance, and logical entailment. His central theme and model is the *impersonal* intellectual satisfaction that a mathematician gets from contemplating a valid proof. Salvation is to go beyond myself, and beyond the personal God, into that impersonal and objective bliss of Reason. But I live in a very different period, after the discovery of time, and I am more-and-more an emotivist. In biology, in history, in the human life-world, and in the world of language in motion, I see all things as coming to be, not by logical necessity, but out of a highly complex interplay of forces, feelings and meanings. That makes my world much *thicker* and less tidy than Spinoza's. It is 'Life', 'the Fray', 'It All': I'm furiously caught up in it, and cannot help but be so in an age as fast-changing and noisily communicative as ours is. It is scarcely surprising that I have taken so long to reach something like stability – and have found some stages of the journey so traumatic.

My conception of the Goal is not as cool, impersonal and exalted as either Spinoza's or the Buddha's. I am still a product of the Christian tradition, and therefore remain more likely to die in anguish like Jesus than 'philosophically', like Socrates. For that reason half of me likes Sartre, Beckett and Miguel de Unamuno, who all saw the human condition as tragic. However much I try to train myself to be solar and to accept universal contingency and transience *intellectually*, when I am hit personally by them I still feel all the old anguish. As we all of us do, of course.[36] Because I take a hotter and more humanistic view of love than either the Buddha, or Spinoza, or any of the long line of celibate philosophers between Plato and Kant, my own intuition of eternal happiness in the midst of transience is bound to be stained with a touch of anguish. That, too, is part of the package, I tell myself. Life is bittersweet. No: it's bitterbittersweet, and religion is to understand and accept that, too. Human love is worth that little bit of pain that it brings with it. Eternal happiness, eternal sadness, both at once, fused together. Be-ings who live in time and subject to chance cannot expect pure and unmixed happiness.

This brief discussion has highlighted the interesting question of what we take the chief aim of religion to be. Different ages have given very different answers. In antiquity religion was often a quest for personal *immortality*. By some act of carelessness or misfortune human beings have lost the immortality that was originally intended for them. For example, the Creator unwisely gave to the dog the task of delivering their new skins to the primal couple. But dogs are well known to be dim, sociable and easily distracted beasts, and the snake had no problem in stealing from the dog our new skins and with them our immortality.[37] And here I have to confess that I don't know of any myth in which we humans really do, or are at least assured that one day we definitely *will*, get those skins back. Instead, there are many tales of a quest for a herb or an elixir of life that will indefinitely postpone death.[38] Daoism in China is full of them. The Christian Eucharist was in early times seen as the *pharmakon* (medicine or drug) of immortality, a claim still not given up. But the recovery of immortality has proved so difficult that it has prompted a rethink

---

36 In Samuel Johnson's *Rasselas*, 1759, a philosopher whose daughter has died totally fails to live up to his own teaching. See Chapter XVIII.

37 An oft-retold African story. Many such stories are very memorable, and make one suspect that they were invented by a gifted individual. There is a Creation-story in which a great black Crow slumbers in pitch darkness, and slowly, slowly, wakes.

38 The Epic of *Gilgamesh* is the best-known.

about the reasons why it was lost in the first place. Perhaps what happened was not merely an oversight or act of negligence, but a major act of disobedience, a *sin* against God?

The idea of sin is most prominent in societies in which the sacred has become very objectified, so that life becomes hedged about by sacred commandments, boundaries, persons, places, rituals and prohibitions. This state of affairs develops in pessimistic times when people fear social breakdown, and a very strong sacred disciplinary framework is felt to be necessary in order to hold human life steady. The fear of God is used to keep people on the straight and narrow path. Transgressions, acts that cross a sacred line, are then perceived as sins that must be punished severely, and the chief problem of religion is to find a way of keeping oneself undefiled by sin. Above all, one needs the *forgiveness* of sins: one wants to die in a state of grace.

Examples of threatened societies in which life became increasingly ritualized and sin became the chief religious preoccupation include perhaps the declining Roman Empire in the West, the Jewish people, always insecure in diaspora, and perhaps conservative Islam today, fighting its last desperate rearguard action against the overwhelming tide of modern Western culture. Today, all the historic faith-traditions around the world are in a state of terminal collapse, and the rise of 'fundamentalism' is certainly not a sign that 'God is back', as journalists say. On the contrary, it is faith in its death agony, struggling to stay alive by the traditional means – objectifying itself, intensifying the consciousness of sin, and conducting a relentless purity campaign against the social pollution caused by homosexuals, abortionists, adulterers, and free women generally.

People in the West are largely unaware of all this. They have already largely forgotten religion and philosophy and they simply lack the consciousness of sin, so that they find the obsessions of fundamentalism baffling. My own view is that we should sympathize with the desperation of the fundamentalists. They behave so crazily because they secretly know that their God is in his death-agony. The next generation, now growing up, will be god-less, and that terrifies them. That's why they are persecuting gays.

They will lose, and religion for most people today is no longer about sin and the struggle to gain the assurance of forgiveness. Today religion is about Chance, Time and Death – about contingency and transience, about the fact that you and I and everyone and everything else is slipping away all the time, and about our lack of anything firm to hold on to. We are all of us falling apart, all the time. I am close to my own extinction: I really am.

Our sudden shock at universal transience is very similar to the young Gotama's reported shock when as a young man he encountered in quick succession an old man, a sick man, and a dead man. But in our case it has been caused by the sudden globalization of cheap communications, and therefore of consciousness, that has happened everywhere since the early 1980s. At that time, the ring of geostationary communications satellites around the Earth was completed. World markets and the conversation of humanity were suddenly globalized. There is now only one human race, and only *one* great debate. The old mutually exclusive local religions and political ideologies have suddenly collapsed. Today, for the first time ever, the principal world religious leaders (I won't name them, but we all know who they are) – they all *know* that it isn't actually *true* any more. They are suddenly ironized: they know it isn't true, but they are obliged to go on talking as if they still think it is true, and therefore an uncomfortable gap has opened up between the views they are institutionally obliged to defend, and what they privately know to be the case. Their plight is unenviable: look at the signs of depression in their frozen, haunted eyes, and the slight tremor of their hands. They know that the news is not good.

It is against this background that my 'systematic theology' has been so austere. We have no choice but to go for a minimalist account of the human condition as it now presents itself to us in late postmodernity. Whether we are thinking about be-ing, or about Big-Bang cosmology and modern physics, or about the strangely evasive and scattering world of linguistic meaning, or about the world of biological life, or about the social presentation of human selfhood – in all areas of life we seem to be losing the old metaphysics of substance (stable, independent being that remains self-identical, and objective, 'absolute', values), and instead find ourselves looking at a temporal process, a flux of events that continuously pours out, scatters, and passes away. Like the motion of thought in our heads, it comes out in a confused rush of tangled language. Briefly it all takes on definite shape, and then it slips away.

In our own case, it appears that our outpouring biological life-impulses, coming out into expression in language, are always not just building the world but also evaluating and interpreting it. In our life-activity the world becomes beautiful and intelligible, and begins to understand itself. But in the endlessly buzzing world of human conversation everything is contested, and everything is continually in process of being renegotiated. The world is lovely, but it is always disputed, and above all it is very *transient*. (And all the more beautiful for that.)

In the old biblical myth, God's function was to show us what it is to be a self who is confronted with a dark and chaotic Other. God showed us how language could impose order, meaning and value upon the flux. In this way, he says, you can appropriate the world to yourself. You can *familarize* it, make it *family*. Now try naming a few beasts, to get yourself started! Oh, and by the way, here's Woman: do you like her? Thus we created God to be what car-designers call an advanced 'concept' or prototype of what we human beings might one day succeed in becoming: and then God, having been enthroned over us by us, duly created us by progressively transferring his own powers to us. Thus God was created by us to teach us how we could become ourselves. Eventually, in radical humanism, we became aware of ourselves as having a special place in the world. Like everything else, we are only out-pouring, scattering process; but because we are highly sensitive biological organisms who have invented language, our own process of self-expression builds the rich, colourful, beautiful world of human life – a world which for the first time in cosmic history is conscious, and begins to understand itself. Before us, before language, the cosmos was so *dark*. It did not know anything about what it was.

Returning now to our contemporary situation in the third Christian millennium, in late postmodernity, I have said that our age is dominated by the mass media, by the continual production and broadcasting of a gigantic volume of information, and by extremely rapid cultural change. In all areas of life we are acutely aware of being completely embedded in, or woven into, a transient process that just pours out and slips away. I am flux. All the old-style certainties, absolutes, substances have simply and finally vanished, leaving us with our own principal religious problem – our acute awareness of transience; that is, chiefly Time and Death. There is no longer any possibility of jumping clear of the process of our life. If we are to find the 'eternal' or 'religious' kind of happiness at all, we must find it in the midst of life, now. And I suggest that we may find it, not just by saying a great Yes to life now, like the Nietzschean superman, but by contemplating a great religious symbol that has the power to reconcile and unify various aspects of our experience, and that can create in us a feeling of eternal happiness in the midst of rushing temporal process. One very apt symbol for this purpose is the Fountain. It stands, perhaps, in the middle of an Italian *piazza* at a place where many ways meet. It swishes, gurgles and sparkles in the sun. People think of it as *lucky*. Why? I guess, because it is blissful to contemplate. The matter of the fountain is nothing but an ever-changing foaming liquid stream, but looking at it is healing and restful. I am reminded of life's unceasing self-affirmation and self-renewal. Nietzsche didn't stress enough the priority of, and the comfort there is *in*, life's spontaneous *self*-affirmation. I feel for the moment simply and completely happy to be part of all this, now. My awareness of it completes life's joy in itself, brings it (once again) full circle.

This then is our working model of a simple, modern and fully up-to-date religion that makes no false claims at all. A religion with no lies, no self-deception and no compulsory untruths that you are commanded to believe. No authorities. Better still, it actually *works*. It gives real consolation.

I don't need to go any further than this. But I still can't help enquiring about the *possibility* of going further. Just now, I was sitting in the sunshine looking at my beautiful Italian fountain and getting my own just-for-now blissful synthesis of pure transience and eternal happiness. Great. But is it possible to go further, and claim that the whole (or the One, or the Absolute) is both utterly contingent and transient all through, and *also* eternal? I mean, really eternally Eternal.

No: I'm not going to claim that. I'm not even going to *think* that, except as an 'as if' (German, *Als ob*). If I am completely happy in the sunshine, now, looking at running water, it is in fact a philosophical mistake to ask for more. I think I should learn to stop at that. Admittedly my late-postmodern world-view is featherlight by historical standards. But I need to recognize that its beauty, its featherlightness, its eternity and my consciousness of it are all one, now, parts of a single package. Best to get that old self-indulgent longing for *more* right out of our heads.

Perhaps our loss is not as great as at first appears. The greatest and most accomplished late work of Latin Christian art is probably the huge Van Eyck altarpiece of 1432, at Ghent. Cast your eye down its mid-line to see how it symbolizes the Centre. At the top, Jesus the Man, enthroned as God. Next down, the Dove descending. Next, the Lamb of God on the altar. Finally, and resting directly upon the earth, is the Fountain of Life.

14

All Over

When human beings first settled and took up farming, they committed themselves to an entirely new way of life, and therewith to an entirely new system of thought. These ideas became the basis of agricultural civilization, and were gradually worked out in great detail. Most people are still clinging to them even today.

For example, they include the following: the Cosmos is a single great rationally ordered system. Its order is most gloriously displayed in its noblest region, the Heavens. The heavenly bodies control events here below on earth. We should live according to Nature. The human mind is – has actually been *made* – capable of comprehending the cosmic order, and making predictions based on it. Astronomy is the first politically important science, for whoever best understands the cosmic order knows how human life and work should be scheduled. Every ruler needs a skilled court astronomer, to help him in drawing up and proclaiming next year's calendar, defining all the dates on which various agricultural tasks need to be performed, markets are to be held, debts paid, and accounts rendered. Human social life and action can thus be planned ahead. As some of our cities copy the shapes of constellations, so our labour must be adapted to the annual cycle of the seasons that is controlled by the sun and the moon. In our Temples, the liturgical calendar reflects the same annual cycle. The religious cycle of feasts and fasts structures time and makes it memorable: we thus know where we are in *time* as well as in space.

You may wonder if we still believe all this. But in England today the newspapers still carry regular small columns of astronomical announcements, and it is quite likely that your desk diary at work still reminds you of the solar solstices and equinoxes, of the lunar phases, and of the times of sunrise and sunset.

Next we notice three great features of this very ancient system of thought: its belief in *a pre-established harmony*, especially between thought and being; its *realism*; and a certain *precisionism*.

In the first place, the old agricultural civilizations always supposed that there was a *pre-established harmony* between the way we humans think and the way the Cosmos thinks itself. The cosmic order is intelligible to us, and our thinking is right thinking when we conform ourselves and our way of life very closely to its rhythm. The intelligible order out there is variously described in terms of Logos, Wisdom, Dharma or Dao, but the idea is always the same: we can participate in cosmic rationality and attune our own life and thought to it; and when we do so, we think and live aright. Our thought is 'orthodox', that is right thought. The Judeo-Christian version of all this vividly declares that God created the human rational soul as a finite image and counterpart of himself, and that is why natural science is possible.

Secondly, since in agricultural civilization the life of human society is conformed to a much grander and pre-existent cosmic order, people's thinking is *Realistic*. It is always assumed that as thought conforms itself to pre-existent being, so language can precisely map states of affairs; and, *specifically*, that the language in which we speak and describe the world is the very same language in which the world is made. God made the world in Hebrew (or in Arabic), and when the heavens 'narrate' – as the Latin Psalm puts it – the glory of God, they do so in Classical Hebrew (or Arabic). Indeed, it is insisted that God himself actually *thinks*, and has from all eternity composed our holy writings, in Hebrew (or Arabic). Nor are such ideas confined to Middle Eastern faith communities: not at all, for Plato himself clearly indicates that the whole intelligible world of eternal Forms follows *exactly* the vocabulary of Attic Greek; and even as late as the seventeenth century it was still being assumed that the modern natural philosopher who works out and describes the order of nature is 'thinking God's thoughts after him'. Even today, most scientists are still realists, in the sense that they assume that the questions they put to the cosmos can and will be answered by the cosmos in the vocabulary of the questioner! Our intellectual at-home-ness in the world continues to be very widely assumed as the background to the average scientist's realism. It's not just that God 'happens' to talk our language: rather, the point is that *he* has expressly made *us* talking *his language*, and able to think as he does.

So much for the thoroughgoing *realism* of the ancient system of thought. Everything's 'out there': we don't make it up for ourselves; we access it by participation. It comes down to us from above, by inspiration or by illumination of the mind, or by revelation. We live by fitting ourselves into an all-comprehending system which is ready-made for us. And if you are yourself still a realist, do notice the point that your sense of the *reality* of God, the world, and the soul is historically an ideological creation, developed in order to keep you bound to the land.

Thirdly, and finally, against this background people have tended to assume, and still do very widely assume, that if we use our language, and perform our ritual and social duties, with sufficient strictness and *precision*, and using a carefully defined vocabulary, then there can be such a thing as *getting It All exactly right*. Hence the traditional dogmatism of theology and of metaphysics in the Judaeo–Christo–Islamic tradition. There is only One Truth Out There: we can get it right in *our* language, and in addition can 'literally' do the Will of God. He has given it to us in writing. All real Truth is basically timeless, because it belongs to God and to the order of Creation as fixed by him in eternity. Therefore the Church teaches the immutability of its own dogma, and most philosophers, having once produced their own system of thought by the time they were 30 or so (or perhaps a bit younger), did not think to change it. Even as late as Schopenhauer, the thinker, having produced his system (aged 28), did not budge thereafter but merely produced little 'parerga and paralipomena' to supplement it. He saw no need to move an inch: he still thought that he had got It All right.

I need not continue, because the whole gigantic scheme of thought, perhaps best preserved and maintained in the West by the Roman Catholic Church, gradually broke down during the nineteenth century. The great prophet of its collapse was Nietzsche, but the *coup de grâce* was administered by Derrida in the 1960s and 1970s. Ways of thinking, deep assumptions that go back several thousand years, were suddenly over.

This sudden today failure of a huge system of thought that served humanity very well for so long is a stupendous event – so big that even today most people remain very reluctant to take it in. For the most part it continues to be thought by the general public that the major threat to traditional religious belief comes from the natural sciences, and in the English-speaking world people are still re-running popular nineteenth-century debates about Darwinism. They are wasting their time. The development of the consciousness of historical change, and especially the history of ideas, since the time of Hegel is far more important. Nietzsche himself started as a classical philologist, and students of his thought cannot fail to notice how important the history of ideas was to him. He is highly (if not always very accurately) aware of the history of social conventions of every kind, especially the history of words; and I think he was the first to recognize, on looking back at the eighteenth and nineteenth centuries, that even the emotions have histories. Today, we have moved on, and even British people recognize the extent to which romantic love was invented in twelfth-century France, humanitarian compassion in early Georgian England, adolescent angst by Goethe, ennui by Stendahl, and being Byronic by Byron. Eventually, everything comes to be seen as a cultural construct, and a product of our own competitive, buzzing conversation among ourselves. Less and less is Originally given, more and more is a matter of interpretation. More and more we come to see the formerly 'real' world as a great arena or theatre in which different schools of interpretation (such as 'conservatives' and 'liberals') are in perpetual dispute with each other. Within this combative conversation, the so-called 'real world' hangs as a fragile, temporary consensus, always only partial, and always shifting.

If it is interpretation, interpretation all the way down, mask behind mask, is there any substrate? What is language's Other, upon which it rides, and which it proposes to form and interpret? I've answered: only outpouring, foaming, gushing, dark, chaotic, empty fleeting contingency, our M/Other. That is why I have said that the starting point for religious thought now is simply transience – which is to say time and death, the universal passing-away of everything, including oneself. And on the account I have given, there can be no One True Faith, and no one correct vocabulary in which one can get It All right. The Fountain has been only one of a number of possible images that might be found helpful in unifying our experience, helping us to accept life, and showing us how we can best live. Other possible images might have been Fire, Life, the Sun and even God. But although I have indeed mentioned God, and Jesus, I have also been careful to avoid any claim that a particular community has been given the franchise and has a special place in the economy of salvation. So: no magical brand-names, not even the name of Jesus.

For almost twenty-five years now I have been trying to illustrate religious thought at work under the new conditions. To this end I have produced a long string of impressionistic sketches, and *not* any big finished academic picture. The sketches make the working visible, and the series of them shows how we and our times change. Since there *is* no ready-made, built-in Truth out there, I could not produce a polished system of thought that might be seen as purporting to be The Truth. We are no longer living in one of the old sacred agricultural civilizations. Our world is only human. All I have ever been able to do is to report the images and considerations in which I have at various times found some comfort and satisfaction. The times are tougher and getting steadily tougher, but this chapter's title is intended to suggest that if we can accept that something great has ended, we may be able to see ourselves as making a new beginning, 'all over' again.

Bibliography

I list here only books expressly referred to in the text and notes, usually specifying the most conveniently available edition.

Benford, Gregory, *Timescape*, London: Gollancz, 1980.

Baudrillard, Jean, *Oublier Foucault*, Paris: Galilée, 1977, ET: New York: Semiotext(e), 1987.

Cupitt, Don, *After All*, London: SCM Press, 1994.

Cupitt, Don, *Solar Ethics*, London: SCM Press, 1995.

Cupitt, Don, *Mysticism After Modernity*, Oxford: Blackwell, 1998.

Cupitt, Don, *The Old Creed and The New*, London: SCM Press, 2006.

Cupitt, Don, *Impossible Loves*, Santa Rosa, CA: Polebridge Press, 2007.

Cupitt, Don, *Above Us Only Sky: The Religion of Ordinary Life*, Santa Rosa, CA: Polebridge Press, 2008.

Cupitt, Don, *The Meaning of the West*, London: SCM Press, 2008.

Cupitt, Don, *Jesus and Philosophy*, London: SCM Press, 2009.

Cupitt, Don, *Theology's Strange Return*, London: SCM Press, 2010.

Cupitt, Don, *A New Great Story*, Salem, OR: Polebridge Press, 2010.

Darwin, Charles, *The Descent of Man*, two vols, 1871.

Darwin, Charles, *The Expression of the Emotions in Men and Animals*, 1872.

Hamilton, G. H., *the Art and Architecture of Russia*, The Pelican History of Art, Harmondsworth: Penguin Books, 1954.

Hick, John, *Evil and the God of Love*, London: Macmillan and New York: Harper and Row, 1966.

Hume, David, *Dialogues Concerning Natural Religion*, 1779, reprinted as Norman Kemp Smith, *Hume's Dialogues*, London: Nelson, 1947, reprinted Indianapolis, Bobbs Merrill, 1962.

Huntington, C. W. Jr, *The Emptiness of Emptiness: An Introduction to Early Indian Madhyamika*, Honolulu: University of Hawaii, 1989.

Kant, Immanuel, *Groundwork of the Metaphysic of Morals*, 1789, translated in H. J. Paton, *The Moral Law*, London: Hutchinson University Library, 1948.

Lawson, Hilary, *Closure: A Story of Everything*, London: Routledge, 2001.

Leibniz, G. W., *Theodicée*, 1710; translated as *Theodicy*, with an Introduction by Austin Farrer, London: Routledge, 1955.

Macmurray, John, *Reason and Emotion*, London: Faber and Faber, 1935.

Magee, Bryan, *The Philosophy of Schopenhauer*, New York and Oxford: Oxford University Press, 1983.

Mill, J. S., *Essays on Religion*, 1874, 'The Utility of Religion'.

Prinz, Jessie L., *The Emotional Construction of Morals*, Oxford and New York: Oxford University Press, 2007.

Riis, Ole and Linda Woodhead, *A Sociology of Religious Emotion*, Oxford and New York: Oxford University Press, 2010.

Spinoza, Benedict de, *Tractatus Theologico-politicus*, 1670; *Ethics, demonstrated in the geometrical manner*, Amsterdam, 1677.

Stambaugh, Joan, *Impermanence is Buddha-Nature: Dogen's Understanding of Temporality*, Honolulu: University of Hawaii, 1990.

Stevenson, C. L., *Ethics and Language*, New Haven: Yale University Press, 1944.

Wittgenstein, Ludwig, *Philosophical Investigations*, Oxford: Blackwell, 1953.